"This must-read book from Annmarie Neal is like having your own dinner party with seven amazing global leaders who offer personal insights on the future of leadership—and no cooking is required."

MARILYN NAGEL
CEO, Watermark

"A must-read for everyone from CEOs, to business school students, to entrepreneurs. Annmarie Neal identifies the essential traits required to lead in today's global economy and turns conventional wisdom on its end to say we need to rethink our current systems to develop global leaders of the future."

ELIZABETH GASPER
Chief Financial Officer, TruEffect

"Annmarie Neal illustrates the social network that drives innovation in business. A must-read for start-up founders as well as multinational leaders."

ALAN COHEN
Chief Commercial Officer, Illumio

"Annmarie Neal defines the leadership traits and actions needed for executives to be successful as the world moves from an international to a truly global and mobile economy. If every candidate read this book, my job would be much easier."

TOM SCANLAN
Spencer Stuart, Global Human Resources Practice

"Annmarie is what I call a 'practitioner thought leader.' She doesn't just do the work, she creates best practices and innovates in the work. Her background as a psychologist gives her a broad perspective and deep knowledge of what makes people and organizations tick...the good and the bad. She's what I call a COCO—a Chief Organizational Capability Officer, someone who can work hand in hand with a CEO to build and develop sustained innovation and organizational capability. In my humble opinion, Annmarie embodies the future of human capital and organizational management, and reading her book provides you with a very valuable insight into that future."

MIKE DULWORTH
President & CEO, Executive Networks, Inc.

"Annmarie Neal has an uncanny ability to take complex issues that face every business today and push the perspective of leaders to adjust their lens toward the future. If you are a leader, *Leading From the Edge* is a must-read to prepare yourself for the changes we see today, but more importantly, to help you stay ahead of the curve for tomorrow."

DANIEL SONSINO
VP, Talent Management Polycom, Inc.

"While many firms invest in executive training programs, few of these programs are truly transformative. What distinguishes the programs that Annmarie Neal documents is the focus on application. Participants spend most of their time learning how to apply a small number of key frameworks. They learn through feedback, which they receive through expert facilitation and personal coaching. The outcome is true transformation in how the participants think about strategic issues and how they act in their leadership behaviors."

DUNCAN SIMESTER
MIT Sloan School of Business

"Annmarie has captured the essence of global leadership, and how to become a global leader, in this incredible book. *Leading From the Edge* is a must-read for every executive and for those who aspire to become one. "

SCOTT OGRODNIK
Silicon Valley High-Tech Executive and Salesforce Transformation Expert

"Edgy read...authentic, thoughtful, and provocative...worth the investment."

DIMITRA MANIS
CHRO, Open Link

LEADING FROM THE EDGE

Global Executives Share Strategies for Success

Annmarie Neal
with Karen Conway

ASTD
PRESS

ASTD Press is an internationally renowned source of insightful and practical information on workplace learning, performance, and professional development.

ASTD Press
1640 King Street Box 1443
Alexandria, VA 22313-1443 USA

Ordering information: Books published by ASTD Press can be purchased by visiting ASTD's website at store.astd.org or by calling 800.628.2783 or 703.683.8100.

Library of Congress Control Number: 2012952832
ISBN-10: 1562868721
ISBN-13: 978-1-56286-872-7
e-ISBN: 978-1-60728-562-5

ASTD Press Editorial Staff:
Director: Glenn Saltzman
Manager, ASTD Press: Ashley McDonald
Community Manager, Global HRD: Wei Wang
Senior Associate Editor: Heidi Smith
Editorial Assistant: Sarah Cough
Text and Cover Design: Marisa Kelly

Printed by: Versa Press, East Peoria, IL
www.versapress.com

Contents

Dedication

To Tucker…
I love you more than chocolate!

Acknowledgments

This project would never have been possible if the leaders involved in this book had not been so generous with their time and insights to share their unique stories. It was their depth of candor and quality of observations about globalisation and leadership that helped inspire our stories and set the course for this book. For this, I want to thank Sanjeev Bikhchandani, Wim Elfrink, Hikmet Ersek, Hannah Kain, Maya Strelar-Migotti, Frits van Paasschen, and Jim Whitehurst. I also want to thank the human resources and communication teams of these executives who extended themselves in support of this project, with particular thanks to Delisa Alexander, Thomas Cherian, Luella D'Angelo, and Eve Dreher.

As editor and collaborator, Karen Conway was instrumental in shaping every chapter of the book. We lived and breathed many of the concepts shared in these pages. Karen translated my vision, helping create value revision after revision. Her dedication was unparalleled: Karen worked tirelessly to move the project from start to finish. We also want to thank Bill Marino for bringing us together and suggesting this partnership, and the ASTD publishing team who brought this project to market.

I would be remiss if I didn't offer my heartfelt gratitude to the several "brains on fire" colleagues and executives who sparked my thinking through the conversations that we've had and through the innovative and courageous work that we've done over the years.

This includes Michael Ansa, Frank Calderoni, Lisa Cavallaro, John Chambers, Shailesh Chandra, Alan Cohen, Marthin DeBeer, Chris Dedicoat, Eve Dreher, Mike Dulworth, Wim Elfrink, Cassandra Frangos, Jim Greene, Ned Hooper, Bruce Klein, Elizabeth King, Brian Koldyke, Robert Kovach, Lieven Lambrecht, Rob Lloyd, Michelle Marquard, Ian Marsh, Angel Mendez, Marilyn Nagel, Ria Nicholls, Scott Ogrodnik, Edzard Overbeek, Duncan Simester, Inder Singh, Faiyaz Shahpurwala, Peter Spanberger, Daniel Sonsino, Matt Tabor, Bill Thomas, Patrick Tse, and Rebecca Zweig.

I want to acknowledge the strategy, innovation, and leadership gurus who've formed my thinking, including Warren Bennis, Clay Christensen, Jim Collins, David Dotlich, Vijay Govindarajan, Gary Hamel, Rebecca Henderson, Sylvia Ann Hewlett, the late Steve Jobs, Bob Johansen, Rosabeth Moss Kanter, Manfred Kets de Vries, A.J. Lafley, Ed Schein, Michael Tushman, Tony Wagner, and the late C.K. Prahalad.

I want to extend special acknowledgment to dear friends and relatives who provided nothing but unconditional support and endless enthusiasm during the highs and lows of this project. Anne Mosley, Barb Schmidt, Darlene Garber, Jillian Parzych, Julie Byerlein, Liz Gasper, Sandy Neal, Sara McBean, Tom Scanlan, and Zeina Daoud—thank you all so much!

To Kermit the Frog, who always reminded me that "It isn't easy being green."

And lastly and most importantly, I want to thank my son Tucker for his endless enthusiasm. There is nothing more encouraging than him saying, "Mommy, you can do it," to keep me motivated. I am so very blessed to have him in my life.

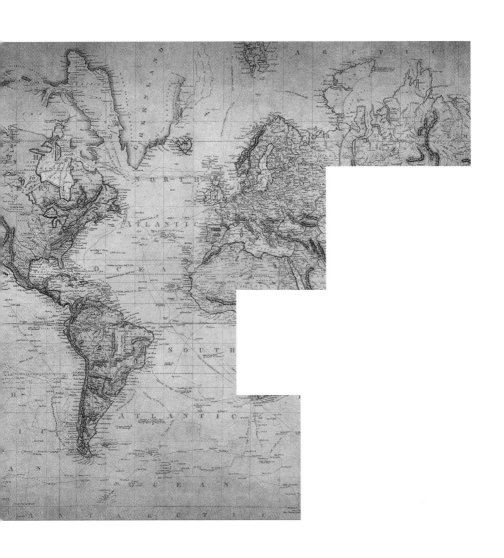

SECTION 1
Context

Introduction

It's not new. It's not unprecedented. But it will have a dramatic, if not decisive, impact on how—and possibly if—you and your business will succeed. Even more surprising, a vast majority of business leaders today are not fully aware that it's happening, the potential impact it could have on their businesses, or what they can and should be doing in response. What's happening is a global shift in capital, in power, and in how, where, and with whom business is conducted, which is shaking the core of what it means to be a global business leader.

As a trained clinical and corporate psychologist with years of experience counseling, consulting, and working alongside thousands of business executives, I have seen firsthand the corresponding shift required by individual leaders and the corporations under their command. Unfortunately, the vast majority of business leaders struggle to make the transition, because they do not recognize the necessity for change. They haven't recognized that the support systems and structures that were successful for them in the past will not work going forward. At the same time, I have also had the pleasure of working with a unique cadre of truly global leaders—many of whom are profiled in this book—who have not only changed themselves and their organizations, but are also changing the world. Through close interaction and observation, I have identified the traits, talents, and techniques that underlie and contribute to their success and from which we can all learn, grow, and fast forward to the desired future state.

As a psychologist, I have explored what contributes to the remarkable nature of these leaders and what prevents others from adapting to today's global business dynamics. I invite you to join me as we explore what will be required of business leaders in a much more connected and information-laden environment and how you can begin building the skills and mindset for success. You won't get the answers from your organizational development team, the curricula at the most prestigious business schools, or even the pages of this book. What you will find by reading on is how to ask the right questions and involve the right people. Along the way, you might just learn something about yourself. Then, and only then, will the answers come and the world be ready to follow your lead.

Most of this book will draw upon my expertise and perspectives as a psychologist and a developer of corporate talent to illustrate what is required for you to succeed as a global business leader. First, it is important to set the world stage, which will put the lessons in the subsequent chapters in context. Context will be a key theme throughout the book, because only by truly understanding the environment in which you are operating can you be relevant— to your customers, your employees, and the broader ecosystem upon which your business depends.

CHAPTER 1

Fast Forward to the Future

THE GLOBAL SHIFT

The current global shift in economic power began relatively quietly about midway through the last century, as the United States' share of GDP began what has been a continual decline from its high of 27 percent in 1950 to just fewer than 20 percent in 2012, according to the International Monetary Fund (2013). You might have missed the trend; many did, especially as investments in new technologies fueled the dot-com driven economic upturn of the 1990s. While the emergence of economic markets in the BRICS countries (Brazil, Russia, India, China, and South Africa) along with places like Mexico and South Korea has not gone unnoticed, the magnitude of their rise in contrast to the slowdown in the U.S. economy is often obscured by U.S. corporations—especially technology firms—that continue to lead the world in innovation and likely will for some time to come. What's overlooked is that an increasing portion of that innovation is occurring in those emerging markets, especially China, India, and South Korea.

Emerging markets are expected to contribute more than half of the global economic growth over the next two decades. The International Monetary Fund reports that the 10 fastest growing economies over the next few years will include the BRICS countries, as well as the secondary markets that support their growth: countries such as Mexico, Malaysia, and the Philippines where abundant workforces are becoming better educated and the political environments are generally favorable to business. The U.S. and Europe, meanwhile, continue to struggle to achieve growth in gross domestic product (GDP) beyond the low single digits, hovering at 2 to 3 percent growth (IMF, 2012).

The Conference Board CEO Challenge Survey 2012 confirms that corporate executives increasingly recognize they are operating in a truly borderless global environment. For the first time since they have conducted the survey, global expansion was included among the top five challenges CEOs say they face. The survey also comments on a new phenomenon: the shift in wealth creation from the developed to the developing world and an increasing reliance on partnerships with smaller to midsize companies in those regions to remain competitive.

It's worthy of note that being on top of the balance of power is not altogether new for either China or India. Think back to what you learned in world history class; according to the World Bank, China and India's share of the world's GDP averaged 50 percent from 1500 through the early 19th century (Maddison, 2001). The shift began as Western Europeans—in particular the Portuguese, Spanish, and British—began to explore and exploit the natural and cultural resources of the East, namely silks and spices. At roughly the same time, the Ming Dynasty, which had been the world's leading economic power, decided to call its enormous merchant marine home and focus domestically instead of internationally. What had begun in Western Europe as a commercial enterprise dependent upon a new and untested view of the world—that it was round not flat—led, although perhaps inadvertently, to the discovery and colonization of what would become the United States and its eventual emergence as a dominant world power.

Fast forward to today, when never before has the world been so flat and yet so large and complex. An insatiable pursuit of new technology, often without a full understanding of its potential power or applications, is propelling a new era of discovery and in many cases, a new world order. The pervasive nature of mobile technology and social networking has increased the size of the network, giving voice (and economic opportunity) to many previously silenced by a lack of connectivity. The complexity of the network has also increased, with many of the new participants following different cultural norms and playing by different rules. For global businesses, these factors necessitate a shift in how, where, by whom, and with whom business is done.

Globalisation in the New World

These shifts are the latest iteration in the evolution of what it means to be a global company. It is no longer enough to design a product in Silicon Valley, manufacture it in Asia, sell it in Europe, and grow value on the U.S. stock exchange. Today, a global company is about more than making or selling products or services globally. There are much broader implications, including how and where you structure your workforce and business partnerships, source materials and vendors, and design and market your products— essentially whatever makes and keeps you relevant in a global marketplace. It's not only how valuable your products and services are to the varied local markets around the globe that you serve, but also how appropriate your organization is, in terms of its structure and operations, to the culture(s) and setting(s) in which you conduct business. The degree of difficulty in staying relevant increases with the number and diversity of markets in which you operate.

Globalisation by companies began centuries ago, with strong government support, for the purposes of colonization and trade. Think Marco Polo and Columbus. Over the years, globalisation evolved, especially in the U.S., to more of a private enterprise, with multinational organizations recognizing that they could offshore non-core business operations (for example, manufacturing and back-shop IT) to achieve specific objectives, such as lower labor costs. While these multinational organizations operated in many markets simultaneously, their predominant center of control for setting strategy, making decisions, and allocating resources remained within the walls and the executive offices of corporate headquarters.

Today, as the economic balance of power shifts, organizations are redefining their global strategies to capitalize on new markets and establish (often literally) closer relationships with their suppliers and customers. While a global company may still have a highly visible corporate headquarters, it doesn't always represent a centralization of power across its portfolio of products and lines of business. Increasingly, more agile global organizations are moving toward distributed centers of excellence and expertise to leverage the human and physical resources of the globe to do work in the best way it can be done.

This was the progressive thinking behind Cisco CEO John Chambers' bold move in 2006 to build a second headquarters in Bangalore, India. By doing so, he believed Cisco could develop products and solutions much closer to the markets for which they are intended, while acquiring top engineering talent from the region. Unlike many other companies, John's globalisation goal was not for cost arbitrage, but rather to better position the company for innovation and growth. Today, Cisco East is home of the company's globalisation center and houses approximately 13 percent of Cisco's worldwide workforce (Aulakh, 2012).

In much the same way that 16th and 17th century European governments sponsored early globalisation efforts, public sector support—this time for education—is helping fuel China and India's return to world standing. In China, Projects 211 and 985 have funneled billions of yuan into an effort to build a network of world-class universities to improve China's research output in the technical and scientific fields. While many challenge the quality as well as reported quantity of four-year professional engineering graduates coming out of China, the country awards the highest number of science and engineering doctorates in the world and is rapidly catching up with the U.S., according to the National Science Foundation (2010). Quality is less in question in India, where the elite Indian Institutes of Technology only accept those ranking in the top 3 percent of the national entrance exam. India also has more investment by U.S. and Indian-based technology businesses seeking to increase the teaching quality at private and smaller Indian engineering colleges. A 2005 McKinsey study found that only 10 percent of Chinese engineering students and 25 percent of their counterparts in India were qualified to work in multinational companies, compared to 81 percent for those graduating from U.S. institutions (Patel, 2010). But when you consider the sheer size of the population base in China and India, even a small percentage can make a difference. A more highly educated population, especially one that knows how to leverage technology, also contributes to the rise of a middle class with disposable income and the corresponding purchasing power of these emerging economies.

A Mobile Makeover

The significance of this transition became strikingly evident on one of my early visits to Bangalore, India. As I rode from the hotel to the office one morning, I watched as literally thousands of people filled the streets, hustling to work or gathering in open air markets to meet with friends. My impression was that despite being the fourth largest technology center in the world (after Silicon Valley, Boston, and London), Bangalore is still very much a third world region, at least by Western standards. Travelling the relatively short distance—10 miles at most—could easily take an hour or longer, with traffic periodically coming to a complete halt to let a cow or two cross the road. Barefoot men used open urinal streams, while mothers simply held diaper-less children away from their hips whenever the babies needed to relieve themselves. Amidst these seemingly impoverished conditions, many of these same men and women were also busy talking on mobile phones. When I got to the office, I asked one of my Indian colleagues about this dynamic. With wide eyes, he smiled and explained, "These people are without the necessities of a Western world, such as shoes and diapers, but they have one of the most important assets: a means to communicate and do business with the rest of the world." That's when I realized that for many, the smartphone has become a lifeline and an instrument of economic development and opportunity.

Consider what the rise in the use of mobile phones in India has enabled. As of May 2012, the country had the world's second largest mobile phone user base, at just fewer than 930 million (Telecom Regulatory Authority of India), which is considerably more than the number of PC users. Wireless communication works for rural India, where 75 percent of the country's 1 billion plus population lives. Global telecom companies have success-fully capitalized on these markets by introducing more affordable phones customized to the needs of rural populations, with localized languages and plans that can be easily shared by multiple users.

By creating easy entry, a company like Reliance Communications, the second largest telecom company in India and a subsidiary of Reliance Global, has quickly built market share and customers. In turn, Reliance and other mobile phone companies have not only created business opportunities for other entrepreneurs interested in serving these previously inaccessible markets, but they have also given those living in these remote regions the chance to market their products and services to the rest of the world. For example, mobile technology can deliver telemedicine services to populations physically isolated from healthcare delivery.

Mobile technology has also created opportunities for more cross border, cross cultural, and sustainable business models. A friend of mine, Shubhra, who used to work sourcing fabrics for Talbots, created *ShubraDesigns* out of a desire to reduce the amount of waste in the production of designer clothing. She buys saris and uses them to create ready-to-wear Western designs out of Asian fabrics, or what she calls "East meets West fusion" fashion.

Thanks to mobile technology and the Internet, she can cost effectively and readily connect with her team in India. She sends her designs to the tailor on his smartphone, and they can discuss any changes before full production begins in New Delhi. Shubhra speaks proudly about using this virtual process successfully to create bridesmaid dresses, emailing both the designs and specific measurements to her Indian team.

A more networked population also creates a much bigger talent base upon which companies can draw, especially as the concept of "going to work" shifts to more of a focus on "doing work." *What* matters more than *where.* People can work at the (business) hub, the club, or the pub—virtually anywhere they happen to be, with equal if not greater degrees of efficiency and effectiveness.

Social Structures

To accommodate and capitalize on this phenomenon, global leaders must take a far more flexible and organic approach to how they grow and structure their enterprises. Over the past 30 years, a primary growth strategy for companies has been to get bigger—often through mergers and acquisitions—in order to produce, at least temporarily, the kind of numbers that Wall Street and other financial markets value. Too often, this approach has led to organizations that are bigger, but not necessarily better at meeting the needs of a global marketplace. Mergers and acquisitions can actually slow down performance, as companies contend with the challenges of cultures and technologies that take time to integrate. This is particularly true for companies with more rigid hierarchical structures. While their focus is diverted, smaller, more agile, and networked competitors can quickly capture market and mind share.

The traditional hierarchical organization worked well in a world for which it was designed: one dominated by industrial processes and requiring both control and standardization. But it can be a liability in an environment where organizations need to outthink and out innovate the competition. Making the transition and giving up control is difficult for many corporate leaders—it goes against what they were taught and what has worked for them in the past. But those who recognize the changing nature of their roles understand the importance of broadening their horizons, their networks, and in some cases, their business models.

Creating a new business model has been instrumental in the success of Red Hat, a leader in open source technology. Red Hat builds software and then gives the code away to a worldwide community of developers—many of whom are customers—who continue to make improvements to the product. The result, says

Red Hat CEO Jim Whitehurst, is better software at a better cost, which increases customer value and, in turn, revenue. There must be something to it; after 40 straight quarters of revenue growth, Red Hat surpassed the $1 billion revenue mark in early 2012, something relatively few technology companies ever achieve.

Whitehurst, who has also succeeded in more traditional business settings (he is largely credited with turning Delta Air Lines around after the 9/11 terrorist attacks), says hierarchical structures were developed in the first half of the last century to control both people and processes. They worked then, primarily because information was limited and took a long time to communicate, which is precisely why they will not work in the information age.

When organizations were rewarded for incremental improvements in productivity and efficiency, their leaders generally knew what to do and how. Today's most successful global business leaders know that their power comes not from what they know, but rather from knowing the right questions to ask and whom to ask. They recognize the value and know how to harness the collective thought power of a much larger ecosystem. This includes those traditionally in their camps: employees, customers, suppliers, and shareholders—as well as other interested parties, such as their suppliers' suppliers and customers' customers, non-governing organizations, advocacy groups, government leaders, and, at times, even their competitors. The traditional roles of these various parties are also changing; think Red Hat and the role that the broader community plays in its products' life cycles.

Advances in collaborative technologies are making it possible for companies to expand the universe of those involved in processes that have been traditionally the responsibility (and privilege) of corporate management. Red Hat routinely uses crowdsourcing to engage its employees, customers, and developers in decision making, which Whitehurst says builds a more engaged and loyal base. But Red Hat is not alone. Crowdsourcing is being used for everything from mission statement creation to new product development. In 2009, Wikipedia drew upon the collective intelligence of more than 1000 online volunteers, all with a commitment to the collaborative content creator's success, to help refine the organization's strategy. But this technology-enabled approach to collaboration is not just for newer tech companies. IBM redefined its culture by conducting a series of jam events in which it asked employees what the company should value (Hempel, 2006). And the 110 year-old manufacturer 3M has used crowdsourcing to identify new opportunities as part of its "Markets of the Future" initiative—a critical input to the company's strategic planning process (Gast and Zanini, 2012).

Social networks and cloud technology offer a host of opportunities for a wide range of companies. Those with widely dispersed workforces can organize and communicate with teams around the world, while smaller companies can scale the computing power they need to grow their businesses. Individual companies are increasingly forming alliances with other firms—sometimes, even competitors—to address specific challenges and opportunities with lower overhead and greater flexibility.

The more ubiquitous, real-time nature of information is also changing the social consciousness of organizations and their leaders. As the social network grows, so does instantaneous access to information about everything you do, as a company and as an individual. Your employees, your customers, and your business partners are interested in more than just whether you make the quarterly numbers. They know and care about value, which goes beyond economics, to incorporate quality: quality in products, in process, and in character. Are your processes and products sustainable? Do you conduct business in an ethical manner? Do you consistently deliver on what you promise? All of these can be challenging for any business, but even more so for global businesses that operate in regions that do not always share the same social or moral codes. In an era of radical transparency, these are not questions that can be answered by your HR or PR teams. As a business leader, you must take much more personal responsibility for how your company, and you as an individual, show up in the world.

Interdependent Thinkers

This requires a fundamental shift in how you think and problem solve. Rather than focus on the long-standing imperative to pursue scaled efficiency (better, faster, cheaper processes), global leaders must become more agile and innovative by pursuing what John Hagel and John Seely Brown, co-chairs of the Deloitte Center for the Edge, call "scaled learning." Scaled efficiency reflected the operational focus of an industrial age. Scaled learning is required to meet the multidimensional intricacies of the global information era (2012).

Complicating matters for the global company is the changing nature of change itself. A business constant for years, if not decades, change has been seen as linear and sequential and applied primarily to process improvement for competitive advantage. Can you do things better, faster, and cheaper than your competitors? Today, if you were to try to depict change, rather than draw a line, you might envision something analogous to vines growing on a piece of lattice. The latticework represents the underlying factors transforming today's global business environment: new enabling technologies, higher education levels within large population bases, and the fall (or at least faltering) of debtor nations. Each of these structures supports the vines, or changes, that intertwine and influence each other's development.

One of the vines represents the emergence of new markets. With new markets come new rules for doing business, and the rules can change depending upon where and with whom you are working. The rules reflect the cultural values and norms as well as the regulatory requirements of different regions and countries, and as such are both informal and formal, but are equally critical to business success. Further, the rules can change over time and have broad sweeping consequences, including how you structure your organizations, compensate your employees, and research and develop new product offerings. The broader your geographic span, the greater the complexity, especially with change occurring simultaneously in multiple regions.

The interdependent and concurrent nature of change creates a multiplier effect. Global leaders and their organizations must continually predict, adapt to, and manage myriad possible outcomes and impacts, resulting in an exponentially higher degree of difficulty. I liken the challenge to playing a multilevel game of chess. Previously, it was enough for business leaders to anticipate how the chess pieces in a single game will move. You might not have known exactly how, where, or when each piece would move, but you understood the parameters and a more defined set of possibilities. Bishops can move diagonally, knights in a figure seven, pawns in any direction—but only one space at a time.

Today, those same business leaders need to play several games of chess at once, each with different pieces and varying rules, all while recognizing that what happens in one game will likely influence what happens in the other games. And with each move, they set the stage for subsequent competitions. This shift requires new ways of conceptualizing, thinking, problem solving, listening, and communicating that have not been historically required of most leaders, and certainly not at this level of complexity. There are also few resources available to teach the skill set, let alone define it.

As a result, today's global business leaders are more like explorers, navigating a world that is changing in an unprecedented manner—not only faster, but on multiple levels and in a far more interdependent fashion. They need to chart new territory, as their business models (even those that have proven successful for decades, if not centuries) may no longer be viable. As global leaders seek to ensure revenue growth while redefining those business models—all against the backdrop of political instability, volatility in the financial markets, and increasing government regulation—they are discovering that their organizational models also need an overhaul. After all, the two go hand in hand. Unfortunately, many organizations are structured to support an economic engine that thrives on control, not originality, and certainly not innovation. Business and organizational models, then, must change dramatically, as we will discuss in more detail in our chapter on innovation. So, too, must the nature of leadership change, and more specifically what is required of successful global leaders. If organizations are to make the required changes to their business models, they will need leaders who are willing and able to change themselves; if not, sometimes the only choice an organization has is to change leaders.

THE LEADERSHIP PARADOX

Contrary to what so many business books and leadership development courses would lead you to believe, there is no magic formula; in other words, you cannot simply follow these 10 steps, learn these skills, or complete this coursework and be on your way. The reason is simple: Learning a step-by-step process assumes the path will continue to be relatively the same going forward. "Walk this way and you will get where you want to be" does not work in a diverse and dynamic world; rather than walk, you might need to swim, or fly, or find an altogether new method to move forward. Sometimes, changing direction is the best course of action, and sometimes you just need to stay in one place, listen, and observe. No one can teach you what to do no matter what the circumstance; the best they can do is help develop leaders who can figure it out as they go along.

Several years ago I had the opportunity to hear Jack Welch, the iconic leader who served as GE's chairman and CEO from 1981 to 2001, speak on the topic of leadership. While Jack and I don't always see eye to eye, he made one point I wholeheartedly agree with: A leader cannot change the game relying only on the leadership behaviors that drove success in the past. When change was more linear, you could learn that if you did X, Y would happen. You could apply what you learned from experience in a fairly predictable manner. Today, there are too many variables for experience to be a reliable teacher. In fact, in some cases, it is exactly what holds some leaders back. The leadership style and skills that worked in a model where efficiency and managerial control ruled may be precisely the things that stifle innovation and growth in an age when creative disruption can be more desirable than predictability.

Most of the tried-and-true leadership models still deployed by organizations today were developed by management theorists who were born at or before the turn of the century. Those models were designed primarily to support manufacturing processes in an industrial age, where the biggest problem was trying to figure out how to do more, faster and more efficiently than your competitors. Processes and management systems were designed by engineers to oversee trade laborers, with control paramount. No wonder they called it the machine age. As the early 20th-century management guru Frederick Taylor wrote in *Principles of Scientific Management*, "The best management is a true science, resting upon clearly defined laws, rules, and principles"(Kiechel, 2012). His thinking sparked a backlash from those who believed that taking such an industrial and restrictive approach to processes that involve people is not only inhumane, but also counterproductive. That tension continues to exist today, especially as more business leaders recognize the need to create an environment where workers are free to innovate, even if those same leaders do not fully understand what it takes to make that happen. We will explore more on creating a culture of innovation in chapter 3.

That's not to say that operational efficiency and productivity are no longer important. They are more important than ever. But the challenge for business leaders today is how to balance the need for day-to-day financial and operational performance (in other words, how to manage core operations, sustain revenue, and keep the stock price steady), all while creating the conditions that will position their businesses to be viable in the future, where the only thing you can count on is that things will be different. For the global business leader, this problem takes on even greater significance because things will not only change over time, but also in relation to the regions of the world in which they operate and the markets in which they serve.

Rather than try to solve this dilemma, one of my objectives in writing this book is to help you think about how to live within this paradox. This is one of many seemingly contradictive positions leaders must embrace. Your role is to help bridge the gap between those who focus on the core management complexities of the business (finance, operations) and those responsible for creating and maintaining relevancy and viability by approaching things differently and on a global scale. While their overall goals may be the same, they speak differently, behave differently, and at times may appear to one another to be acting in a manner that, at best, seems irrelevant and, at worst, contradictory to their respective objectives. Global leaders must become the glue that keeps their organizations moving forward holistically, while allowing these various actors to play the roles they perform best.

SECTION 2
The Essential Traits

CHAPTER 2

Essential Traits 1-3

Over the years, serving as a management consultant and as the corporate lead in charge of executive development, I have assessed and developed thousands of leaders, most of whom were either preparing for or already in significant global assignments. Working closely with these individuals, I have learned that there are certain notable traits that distinguish those who hold global positions from those who are truly (deep in their being) global leaders. Interestingly, the differences have little to do with age, gender, where they were raised or schooled, and even the kind of on-the-job training they received or the number of countries stamped in their passports. These are certainly important factors that contribute to one's ability to do global work; they provide the playground in which budding leaders can learn and grow, but they do not make a global leader. What I have found is that the true differentiating qualities are more psychographic than demographic in nature.

Psychographics is a concept that has been fully embraced by marketing professionals in search of the differentiating factors that will determine the likelihood of someone buying a particular product or service, joining a group, or contributing to a cause, regardless of more traditional qualifiers such as age, economic status, and even education level. A slightly tongue-in-cheek description comes from Stephen G. Barone with Barodine Marketing in a 2010 article where he discusses how to reach people who are more prone to buy extended warranties for their small appliances. While he quips that there are apparently "many people quietly walking among us who are anxious about the sudden catastrophic failure of their toaster ovens," he explains that the key to developing a successful marketing campaign is in understanding a person's psychographic profile, which in this example is probably "more risk averse [and] pessimistic" than the small appliance purchasing population at large. If you understand their psychographic traits, you can better predict their tendencies to think, feel, or act in a certain way, and in turn you can craft messages that are more relevant to them. As Barone explains in his article, you might capitalize on their pessimistic nature by reporting on the increasing likelihood of appliance breakdowns over time and how the extended warranty will protect them from unexpected expenses.

Marketing aside, I have found that there is a unique psychographic profile for the truly great global leaders I have had the opportunity to observe and work alongside. The differences present themselves in how these leaders think, how they gather and synthesize information about the world around them, and as a result of how they influence and energize others. While there is no recipe for success, I have found that those executives who are best positioned to lead on a global scale possess certain essential traits that are relevant regardless of the kind of organization they lead, the sector in which they operate, the markets where they are located, or whether they are in established or relatively new businesses or industries. These are not so much a set of skills as they are a way of *being* in a much larger, more connected, and more volatile world. Leading is more about who you are, as opposed to what you do, but who you are will influence how you approach the world, the decisions you make, and ultimately how well you perform as a leader. Those leaders who possess the essential traits described below are much more comfortable on the edge. To them, living and leading on the edge is not precarious; it's an adventure of ideas and opportunities that can only be realized if you are willing to challenge yourself and your organization to take that next step. Not blindly, mind you, but rather with eyes wide open, which begins with Essential Trait #1.

THE ESSENTIAL TRAITS

Essential Trait 1:
A Strong Sense of Self

An unusually astute sense of self translates into an ability to understand the world and the people around you on many levels and in many different contexts. It's as if executives with this trait know their place in the world, and their place is to create something new, something different, something very, very good. Purpose coupled with a powerful strength of conviction keeps these leaders pushing forward even in the face of obstacles or when pressured by others to do something else, while never forgetting their responsibility to satisfy the needs of the board, shareholders, customers, or employees. It's as if their sense of purpose is so great that they can block out criticism in a manner that allows them to move forward with courage and determination. They move with a single mindedness but without being blind to cues that would indicate they may need to adjust or change course. As such, they do not close themselves off to better ideas or new ways of doing things. While it may sound trite, they attribute greater meaning to their own existence and are able to provide meaning to their companies, their employees, and even customers, with significant results. You will see this for yourself when I introduce you to some of our highlighted executives in section IV.

These global leaders have big visions coupled with equally big plans and a determination to set their own course without needing the approval of others. At the same time, they have what I consider a different kind of psychological freedom that allows—and in fact almost requires—that they continually question and challenge the status quo, even their own way of thinking, being, living, and leading in the world.

This is one of many dichotomies that global executives embody. On one hand, they are firm in their convictions and what they believe to be right. And yet, they have no borders when it comes to their aspirations and to their exploratory and inquisitive natures. When *Fortune* magazine described Amazon CEO Jeff Bezos as "the ultimate disruptor," he took exception. In a November 2012 interview with Charlie Rose, Bezos instead called himself more of an inventor and an explorer. Disruption, he said, is just a consequence of a good invention. Bezos extends his personal sense of self to Amazon's culture, which he describes as a "pioneering, explorer mentality" (Rose, 2012). Apparently it works, with what started as an online bookseller in 1994 now a $100 billion company "pushing into everything from couture retailing and feature film production to iPad-worthy tablet manufacturing" (Lashinsky, 2012), not to mention the 30 percent jump in stock price in 2012.

I saw the same dynamic a few years ago when I was working with John Chambers, the CEO of Cisco Systems. John firmly believed Cisco could change the world, first through networking and subsequently with collaborative technologies. His confidence in the life-changing nature of these technologies underscores the company's mission statement: to change the way the world works, lives, learns, and plays. While the company sold hardware and software solutions, the employees were on a mission to change the world. They were inspired by John's relentless enthusiasm and buoyed by his impressive ability to accurately predict market transitions. But Chambers' success, and that of many leaders of his caliber, comes from more than just being smart and charismatic. I believe it starts with a confidence in knowing that what you are doing is right, that it matches where the world is going, followed by a relentless pursuit to see if there is something different, something better. Then, once you have found it, insist on looking just a little further, around the corner, over the edge, to see if there is something really different and much better. This attitude permits people and entire organizations to think more freely (beyond their own intellectual inhibitions) about what's possible and inspires them to make it happen.

Finally, these leaders have a unique cadre of coping skills. They are more resilient than most, but they also have the emotional maturity and insight to differentiate and stay focused on what's most important. They know which battles to fight and which to leave well enough alone. Perhaps most importantly, they have a sense of humor that is both adaptive and healing. They can, and often do, laugh at themselves. As a result, while they have big egos—they have to in order to take on the challenges they choose—they are able to use humor to moderate what could otherwise be overwhelming personalities. Yet another enigma is their "go big or stay home" attitude, coupled with an honest assessment of themselves and a sensitivity to the impact they have on others. Are these exceptional global leaders motivated differently from others, even others in comparable positions? That has been my observation. Their ambitions, both personally and for their organizations, exceed that of the "average" leader, as if you could say that the head of any multinational company is ever average. The difference is their degree of tolerance for the risks associated with their aspirations. It's not that they aren't afraid. Of course they are—sometimes very afraid. They are human. But it is almost as if they are motivated by their fears, rather than paralyzed by them. They have a certain "bring it on" quality that is truly remarkable—and truly distinguishing.

I cannot emphasize enough how important it is to "know yourself"—who you are, what you stand for, what motivates you, what is most important, and what is non-negotiable. Working globally will challenge anyone's business standards, ethics, and moral constitution on a daily basis. Global leaders that successfully run this gauntlet have an internal compass that guides them toward the appropriate behavior, for themselves and their companies, even when that behavior may not be in line with their personal preferences or traditional values. There may well be times when they need to adapt their approach depending on the social and cultural context, but they have the ability to do so without compromising their core values.

N.R. Narayana Murthy, one of the founders of Infosys Ltd., the Indian-based business consulting, technology, engineering, and outsourcing services company, was an exemplary leader in this regard, most notably for standing up against political corruption in his home country. A fundamental component of his platform as CEO was to change the way business was done in India. He set high standards for Infosys and held firm in the face of many, many obstacles. Unlike other global leaders who often go to extra lengths to avoid business models that rely on government involvement, Murthy took it on. He was able to do so because he and the other founders had agreed to create a values-based organization with the vision to be India's most respected company, delivering best-of-breed technology solutions and employing best-in-class professionals. But we all know that a vision statement in and of itself isn't enough—leadership must act in ways that set the right tone and reward the right actions. As an example, he often tells this story: In 1984, Infosys imported a super-minicomputer to develop software for overseas customers. When the machine arrived at the Bangalore airport, the local customs official refused to clear it, demanding a bribe. Instead, Murthy insisted on paying a 135 percent customs duty. The company had to borrow the money to pay the tax, but Murthy felt that if Infosys was to do business ethically, it did not have a choice (Raman, 2011).

Essential Trait 2: Multimodal Thinking

The next trait is what I call multimodal thinking. Many of the truly exceptional leaders I have met and worked with possess a rare capacity to rapidly absorb, synthesize, and organize information that helps them understand the world around them, even when that world is radically different from what they have experienced before. Almost simultaneously, they are able to use that new worldview to determine how best to lead themselves and their organizations going forward. This multilevel processing enables them to respond more quickly and effectively to market changes and opportunities.

For many people, being in the presence of a multimodal thinker is a bit like watching a magic show. You don't know how they do it, but you know it works. They are able to conjure up a new idea or insight, if not from thin air, then from seemingly disparate pieces of information and usually from different sources. A senior technology executive whom I once coached was particularly adept at using multimodal thinking to reach strategic conclusions. He could sit in a room with customers, partners, and colleagues and make connections that few in the room could otherwise see. It was almost as if he floated over the top of a conversation, pulling out what he considered to be the most salient points. By itself, each point may not have seemed incredibly relevant, but by considering them together, this executive was able to bring an entirely new level of thinking (and insight) to the conversation. Even more impressive, he could apply this approach to multiple conversations on multiple topics with multiple audiences, linking each of them together to derive even more profound insights. Sometimes it was simply— although this is anything but simple—a matter of taking something that came out of one conversation and applying it to a different context, market, challenge, or opportunity. Other times, the insights that arose from each respective conversation contributed to an entirely new revelation. No matter the pathway, the result was the ability to put forth a "disruptive" conclusion, from which a never-before-thought-of strategy could be developed. For those of us who study how the mind works, this executive has the distinguishing capability to recognize patterns.

Pattern recognition, in my opinion, may be one of the most critical success factors for global leaders (the second being the ability to sleep on airplanes). It is the ability to recognize the interconnections and relationships between seemingly disparate data points and synthesize that information to formulate overarching themes. One who can pattern recognize never loses the forest for the trees. The more relevant the data and the faster someone can recognize the patterns, the more valuable the skill.

Now, couple this with the ability to think in a multimodal manner. Multimodal thinkers look at a problem and the causal relationships between a wide range of variables associated with that problem, such as market needs, competitors, product capabilities, cost, the regulatory environment, new technologies, and even social and cultural values. Where more linear thinkers need to break down highly complex problems into bite-sized pieces, multimodal thinkers have the ability to see something all at once and as a whole. In other words, they can see what is, complete with all of the factors that could potentially influence the situation and the outcome, which enables them to consider problems in a much larger context and to search for solutions more extensively, even beyond what is considered possible.

Multimodal thinking is a more complex form of integrative thinking, a concept first identified and defined by Roger Martin, dean of the Rodman School of Management at the University of Toronto. In his research, he interviewed dozens of successful global leaders, including GE's Jack Welch, former Procter & Gamble CEO A.G. Lafley, and Infosys co-founder Nandan Nilekani, to understand their respective approaches to problem solving. The common characteristic he identified helps explain the many enigmas associated with truly global leaders. It is "the predisposition and capacity to hold two diametrically opposing ideas in their heads, and then without panicking or simply settling for one alternative or the other, they're able to produce a synthesis that is superior to either opposing idea" (Martin, 2007).

Edzard Overbeek, senior vice president of services for Cisco Systems, is an exceptional integrative thinker. When determining the best way to innovate the business model for the Asian theater—a region where Cisco is under significant competitive assault from the likes of the Chinese company Huawei—Edzard looked beyond the core go-to-market strategy of selling routers and switches, which are commodity hardware products. Instead, he moved "up the stack," proposing partnerships with a wide range of organizations, some of whom were competitors, some collaborators, and many both. He understood how Cisco complements others and vice versa, without ever losing sight of the competitive nature of the relationships and, more importantly, the ultimate value they could deliver together. As a result, Edzard was able to position Cisco much higher and more prominently in the value chain. This might sound simple, but to reach these conclusions, Edzard and his team had to look at Cisco's suite of offerings from a customer-centric vantage point, including identifying different segments for which specific innovations and solutions features would appeal the most. The team looked at different kinds of data and connected the dots in different ways than other industry competitors were considering at the time. And in doing so, the team developed customer solutions that would ultimately provide longer-term value to Cisco. This ability to "connect the dots" is a critical component of innovation that we will explore in chapter 5. As Apple founder Steve Jobs was often quoted as saying, "Creativity is just having enough dots to connect." I would add that it is also the ability to hold all the dots, even those that are seemingly contradictory, together to create a new whole.

There is an iterative process of moving back and forth between various ways to look at an issue or a problem: how to define the problem, the relationship between the variables, the possibl connections or architectures that underlie the relationships between the variables (pattern recognition, once again), and finally how decisions (ideally more innovative and creative) are reached. There is an appreciation of the natural tensions between variables and a curiosity of how these variables come together. Integrative thinkers recognize the relevancy of things others might miss, such as when there are contradictions between what a customer says, (for example, they like this feature or that) and how they behave (how they actually use the product). Integrative thinkers bring it all together by synthesizing and translating salient information into simple insights that ultimately lead to new solutions.

This ability to make connections and interconnections across industries, technologies, markets, and geographies is an incredibly important skill for the global leader. It is essential to the process of developing strategies and collaborative relationships that keep a company, even an entire industry, relevant over the long term.

I witnessed a verbal analogy for multimodal thinking when working with a Pan-European leader who spoke seven languages fluently. Her team was also multilingual. When they worked together, the members would move from one language to the next, choosing the words and phrases in the language that best described what they were attempting to communicate and the problem they were trying to solve. In other words, they did not allow themselves to be limited by the constraints of a single language, a single way of thinking, a single meaning, a single cultural interpretation. There were no cognitive boundaries between languages, and when asked, most would say they didn't even realize that they were switching languages. They just found the best way to express their thoughts and spoke as such. Multimodal thinking does this but at a higher level, across several cognitive, psychological, interpersonal, and social variables simultaneously, and ideally, as in the case of the Pan-European leader and her team, without the need for translation.

This situation is unfortunately unique. All too often, the individual who has that critical ability to think multi-dimensionally and recognize patterns often struggles to communicate his revelations in a manner that non-multimodal thinkers can understand and more importantly act upon. If you fall into this category, do not despair; it does not prevent you from succeeding. You can complement your skill sets by ensuring you have people on your team who can translate your insights into the linear thinking and operating world.

I had to laugh recently (although while beaming with pride) when my son's 4th grade teacher wrote in his report card: "Tucker is most successful when reflecting, making connections, and making predictions. He needs to work on explaining his thinking when asked questions or deciding something is important by providing more evidence to support his ideas." We will explore how business leaders can employ the use of what I call "value translators" to overcome similar challenges in chapter 5 on innovation.

Think back to the multilevel chess game analogy I used before. The multimodal thinker can skillfully play several games of chess at once, while continually recognizing that each move not only shifts the game that is being played but also other games underway at the same time. As a result, your strategies need to be multidimensional and easily adaptable.

In the game of business, the same is true. The multimodal executive thinks and operates on several levels, recognizing that what works in this geographic region or regulatory environment, as an example, may not work elsewhere, and all the while, never losing sight of the entirety of his business and the larger ecosystem in which it exists. While this may sound obvious, for many leaders it is surprisingly not. It takes significant intellectual capability and endurance to hold all of these components together in a meaningful way and with equal rigor and cognitive commitment.

To put these concepts in more concrete terms: They are survival skills. Given the vast amounts of information that cross an executive's desk, how does one skim and pull out what's most meaningful and then recognize how they relate to one another, something that is essential to effective strategic planning. No doubt, one must be able to analyze data—about markets, customers, competitors, and technology—in great detail. But it is the process of generating meaning beyond the data itself that paves the way for new value creation.

Essential Trait 3:
Courage to Re-create
Everything, Including Yourself

The third essential trait is in knowing when that which has worked in the past is destined for failure going forward. The dilemma faced by many leaders is that when they find a good model, say Dell's "Build it to Order," they have a hard time letting go. For global leaders, this dilemma is amplified, given the need to operate multiple business models simultaneously around the world. Truly global leaders need the intellectual acuity to know what to keep, what to destroy, and what to re-create across their organizations, in order to remain relevant to myriad markets and constituents. More importantly, they need the emotional intelligence and the mettle to take action, especially when what must be destroyed is exactly what made them successful in the past.

How is it that once-successful companies so often lose their footing? Management guru Peter Drucker addressed these questions in a 1994 *Harvard Business Review* article entitled, "The Theory of the Business." In it, Drucker says they are acting upon the wrong assumptions, "assumptions that worked once but no longer fit reality," whether they are about markets, customers, competitors, technology, or the company's strengths and weaknesses. As he so succinctly explained: "These assumptions are about what a company gets paid for." And if they are the wrong ones, the company doesn't get paid.

So how do you keep those assumptions and in turn your organization strategically relevant? The answer is relatively simple, although the process (starting and sticking with it) can be challenging. Leaders who remain the most relevant are those who constantly review and refresh everything about themselves and their organizations. It's easier said than done, but it is those leaders who take personal responsibility to make this part of their companies' ethos who not only survive, but thrive, in a changing marketplace.

Too often, I see leaders failing to achieve market or leadership potential because they don't have the courage to fully re-create their organizations, not just rearrange the deck chairs on the Titanic. The courage to re-create refers not only to the business model, but also to the organization, the culture, and even leadership teams. Many of the most well-intentioned leaders have the insight and courage to change one of these elements, but they fail to reach beyond and substantially change the other elements as well. As a result, they might put forth a highly relevant market strategy, but without the necessary culture or organizational structure or leadership team in place to execute. After a few years, they sit back and wonder why their strategy did not produce the intended results.

...Your Business Model

It is not uncommon for organizations to wonder how their business models that were so successful in the past are no longer producing acceptable results. They face what I call "the crisis of what's next," in which they worry about how their current business models will help them capture new markets and thrive in new economies. Alternatively, your company may suffer from the "crisis of success." Certainly Dell did and is now investing millions upon millions of dollars to reinvent what was once a highly respected and envied value proposition, just to remain competitive in what has become a commoditized market.

Borders is another classic case. How is it that Borders was forced to shut its doors when its near identical twin, Barnes and Noble, remained a viable enterprise? Easy, because Barnes and Noble continued to challenge its core business model, while Borders was unable or unwilling to let go of its once competitive advantage: the ability to hold massive quantities of inventory in its stores. Both companies pioneered the mega-bookstore concept and moved into selling music, video, and even coffee. But while Borders invested in its physical stores, Barnes and Noble recognized the impact Amazon was having in the market and shifted its focus to online sales and e-books. It even created its own e-reader, the Nook, to compete with Amazon's Kindle. Borders filed for bankruptcy in February 2011, while Barnes and Noble continued on. That's not to say the company does not face fierce competition, especially in light of Amazon, which has once again disrupted the business model— this time by pricing its expanding line of Kindles not to make money but to generate revenue through increased e-book downloads. But that's a whole other story.

Here are a couple examples of other companies that have successfully reinvented their business models:

Netflix vs. Blockbuster

Netflix remains relevant by disrupting its own business model. The company began in 1997, shortly after one of the founders, Reed Hastings, personally experienced a market pain point when he had to pay $40 in late fees on a movie rental. Hastings recognized the potential for using an emerging technology, the DVD, to address the problem. A year later, the fledgling company began offering DVDs by mail.

Blockbuster, the once dominant player in the home-video market, first tried to fight the upstart Netflix with a lawsuit claiming that the company's revenue-sharing agreements with movie studios hurt competition. The lawsuit was later dismissed, and Blockbuster finally gave into the trend in 2002, buying an online DVD rental company and offering unlimited movie rentals with no late fees. But it had taken too long. That same year, 2002, Netflix founders had already publicly announced plans to offer a better alternative—streaming videos—even though they had yet to turn a profit with the original business model. They were always looking ahead. The company made good on its plans, introducing video-on-demand via the Internet in 2007. Meanwhile, Blockbuster remained in denial, with CEO Jim Keyes stating as late as 2008 that he's "been frankly confused by this fascination that everybody has with Netflix." Two years later, Blockbuster filed for bankruptcy protection.

Netflix also knows how to fail fast, another essential trait we will discuss later in this chapter. The same year that Blockbuster revamped its approach, 2002, Netflix opened a brick-and-mortar DVD rental store in Las Vegas, only to close up the physical shop in less than a month.

LEGO®—More Than a Child's Game

After experiencing revenue and profit losses since 1998, the Danish niche toy manufacturer LEGO® was on the edge of ruin in 2004. CEO Jorgen Vig Knudstorp knew he had to dramatically change the company's business model. In addition to a concerted focus on improving product development and production, LEGO® undertook an aggressive diversification plan, expanding its business beyond the traditional interconnecting building blocks to include a new line of clothing, theme parks, and video games. LEGO® is cool again. There is even an "Art of the Brick" travelling museum exhibition focused exclusively on the use of the LEGO® bricks as an art medium.

...Your Leadership Team

Being able to recognize what kind of capabilities you need on your team is another sign of true leaders, but it also has to come with the courage to go deep into the market, to find those who have those competencies and to hire them. Don't worry if someone is smarter or better than you. My advice: If they are smarter, if they are better than you, hire them now. Do not pass "Go." Do not collect your $200. Stop what you are doing and hire them. This is particularly challenging for the leader who has built a team of loyal partners who have contributed to the organization's success in the past but who may no longer be well-suited for where you need to go in the future.

It gets even more difficult when you worry about how your current (been with you since the beginning) team members will feel about having new blood on the team. For years, I have not been able to crack this nut. I have worked with some of the smartest and most successful leaders in industry. They command the attention of their competitors and the capital markets, and yet they have blind spots around talent. Even in the face of robust analytical (hard) data, they will overrule logic for loyalty. A leader's job is to make the tough decisions and have the courage to attract and help assimilate new players who will challenge the status quo, day after day, in order to keep the company's thinking fresh.

Recently I consulted with an organization, which will remain nameless for what will become obvious reasons. The company was well positioned: It had a strong and market-relevant product with a defensible patent that protected those aspects that were unique to its intellectual property. The company also had the benefit of fully engaged investors with deep pockets who were willing to put their weight behind the technology play. The trifecta came in the form of good advisers on the board, ready to bring their experiences (as well as those of their companies) to bear. And yet, the CEO was unwilling, and perhaps even unable, to re-create his organization to meet shifting market demands. It wasn't for lack of support. As I just mentioned, this CEO was completely surrounded by resources and capital to make the necessary changes to meet current and future market demands. The CEO was psychologically constricted by his own limits—maybe out of fear, perhaps out of not knowing the right answer, or possibly out of pure stubbornness that he was the only one who had the right answer. Bottom line, he did not have the courage to do what was necessary, including making some strategic changes to his leadership team. Even as new talent was brought into the company, this CEO remained loyal to an old guard who did not have the skills or sensibilities to succeed in a highly dynamic business environment. Not only did the company fail to anticipate some major technology trends, but it also created a toxic environment for employees. As others watched the mistakes being made, they became highly discouraged; they were not empowered to fix the situation, and they questioned why those who had made the mistakes were allowed to remain in power.

In one year, the company went from a viable market player with strong customers, including Match.com and H&R Block, and a viable exit strategy to a flailing business that missed significant market transitions (such as the move to mobile). It would not reach its potential under the current CEO. The board eventually replaced this CEO with an entrepreneurial leader who will hopefully bring fresh thinking and new blood needed to turn the company around. As we will explore further in chapter 5, sometimes a change at the top is the only way to change a company's course. This under-scores the importance of having the right leader, with the right qualities (although not necessarily all the answers) at the helm.

Why does this happen? Sometimes I think it is over-confidence in one's own "smarts." Some executives, frankly, are not insightful enough to appreciate that they don't know what they don't know. Just because you are the most senior executive doesn't mean that you are the smartest person in the room. And even if you are, it doesn't mean you are the best person to solve a particular problem. That's why, as I have emphasized before (and will again) it's important to have the right team around you and to respect their judgment and individual and collective strengths. Also, what worked in the past will likely not work in a global marketplace that is volatile, uncertain, complex, and ambiguous (VUCA). VUCA is a term first coined by the military that is increasingly used by businesses to describe the need to make decisions in an environment that carefully considers both current and future states. To do so successfully, companies must appreciate the interdependence of variables in order to understand the potential consequence of their actions and identify relevant opportunities.

VUCA is behind Unilever's initiative to double the size of its business in 10 years while reducing the environmental footprint and increasing its social impact. As chief marketing and communication officer Keith Weed described it, "We look at the world through a [VUCA] lens...you can say, 'It's a very tough world,' or you can say, 'It's a world that's changing fast, and we can help consumers navigate through it.' Two-and-a-half billion more people will be added to the planet between now and 2050, of which 2 billion will be added in developing countries. The digital revolution, the shift in consumer spending—all this suggests that companies have to reinvent the way they do business"(2012).

The fact is, you can't be strategic as a leader or an organization unless you can manage and thrive in a VUCA environment. Now, get to work on creating what will work in the future! And don't forget to look where you are going: The future is in front of the windshield, not in the rearview mirror.

...Your Culture

Corporate cultures often need to be reinvented as well. But it is around culture that many executives slip up. Because it is so hard to quantify, they place it lower on their priority lists. Caroline J. Fisher, PhD, who writes extensively on corporate culture as it relates to bottom-line business performance, describes their thought process as: "If I can't define it, can't measure it, can't change it, and am unclear how it links to results, why bother?" (2000). But she says it can and should be linked to results, because it is so closely aligned with behavior. It's why I have so often counseled executives that it is up to you to take responsibility for your company's culture and lead by the example of how you want your employees and your company to behave. After all, just because your strategy demands it, doesn't mean your culture will allow it. We will explore this more in chapters 5 and 6.

...Yourself

The fastest way to change a culture is to change the leader, but that doesn't mean the leader has to go. Ideally, she will make the conscious and purposeful decision to make the personal changes necessary to set the stage for a culture of success and innovation. Unfortunately, when people are in an uncertain environment, their tendency is to retreat to that which is known and comfortable and not take risks, especially when it comes to their own persona. In those cases, sometimes the only option is for the company to make the difficult decision to forcibly remove the leader, which can be extremely unsettling for the entire organization. That's why leaders who re-create themselves—or at least have the insight that they need to—create the environment that makes it easier for organizations to navigate the challenging but necessary change process.

Earlier, I introduced you to Edzard Overbeek, a strong-minded Dutch executive with a remarkable capacity for self-reflection and transformation. I first met Edzard when he was in his late 30s and running a fairly large business operation for Cisco in Europe. When the company offered him the opportunity to take an expanded assignment as leader of the Japan division, he put himself into the assignment fully, taking responsibility for the personal change that would be required for a Dutchman to succeed in a highly homogenous culture, vastly different from that which he was accustomed to in Europe. He learned the language, he embraced and mastered the nuances of the culture, he engaged the people. Most importantly, he fully (and honestly) reflected on how he would need to change his own thinking, style, and historically European approach to management. It took courage to command the team while he was still adapting to the cultural requirements of the market and the organization, to uproot what had worked for him before and re-create himself in the face of these new leadership demands. Edzard not only courageously re-created himself in Japan, but also later when he became the president of Cisco's entire Asian operation. And he is doing it again today, as the newly named leader of the company's large services business in the United States.

This executive and other successful leaders exhibit what my longtime mentor Warren Bennis calls "adaptive capacity." In their book *Geeks and Geezers*, he and co-author Bob Thomas describe five basic qualities that their research on multi-generational leaders found to be organic to the ability to lead. They define adaptive capacity as "the ability to process new experiences, to find their meaning, and to integrate them into one's life—the signature skill of leaders and, indeed, of anyone who finds ways to live fully and well."

Psychologically speaking, those with the capacity and willingness to adapt have an underlying disposition to exploration, to question not only the relevance of their organizations and their respective business and revenue models, but also their own leadership styles and that of their closest and often most loyal team members.

It takes courage to re-create. You have to stop "doing" long enough to look in the mirror and ask: "What does it mean to be a leader? What is the essence of my leadership style and, more importantly, my platform? What do I stand for? And what does this mean for the organization I lead and the people who follow me, whether they are employees, customers, business partners, or part of the society at large?"

Tough questions, but when you have a greater sense of self (remember Essential Trait #1) and know how you relate to the world, you can overcome obstacles that may be holding you back in order to unlock your potential for leadership. The irony here is that only by knowing who you are today can you become who you need to be tomorrow. The essential traits, as you will continue to discover, are closely interconnected and complementary in nature.

Personal re-creation is the most challenging but often the most rewarding, personally and professionally. Here are some true stories to inspire you.

The Guilt Trap

I was brought in to coach a strong product development engineer viewed by the organization as one of the highest potential young managers on the senior operating team. They saw it, but he didn't, and his lack of personal insight into his own potential repeatedly held him back. In fact, he would often undermine his own success. He had risen to various management positions as the result of his raw intellect and ability to problem solve, but then he stopped progressing. When faced with significant market competition, he would hold back and manage to the limitations of the senior team, rather than rise above. He knew the right questions to ask, but he wouldn't ask them. He had some of the most creative approaches to tough problems, but he wouldn't share them. By exploring these issues with him, I learned he was the oldest child of several siblings, each of whom had different fathers. Their mother struggled with drugs. He managed to get into a good college and land a quality position, thanks to some mentors along the way who encouraged him to work hard, but once in the work environment, he struggled. By working together, we discovered that he was feeling guilty for moving ahead of his siblings and was unconsciously holding himself back. Once he understood this dynamic, he was able to move forward and fully realize his potential as a leader and executive. He moved into very senior roles in the company and remains a strong leader to this day.

Change on Purpose

A highly regarded and successful operations director with a lengthy track record for driving project plans to fruition continually sought advancement at every opportunity. She was repeatedly promoted to projects of increasing scope and global complexity. She would excel with key project deliverables only to be rewarded with bigger and more challenging problems to solve. But something always seemed to be missing for her. She enjoyed her work and the results that she achieved for her organization. Her assignments took her around the globe, meeting interesting people and delivering key projects across multiple cultures. But she was repeatedly frustrated by the fact that although she consistently delivered, she was never considered for promotion to vice president.

She was nominated to participate in a company-sponsored executive development program for high potential, emerging leaders. This program gave her the opportunity to not only work on an important strategic initiative for her company but also to explore who she was as a leader (and as a person), and more importantly what she truly wanted to achieve in her profession and in her life; in other words, to explore her passion and her purpose. At relatively the same time, this executive also faced some major changes in her personal life. While challenging, they actually made her more disposed to exploring what she truly wanted and to setting herself up for transformational change.

In the program, we challenged this executive's assumptions about what success meant to her. She came to the conclusion that she was not being true to herself and pursuing her dreams. She was doing good work, but it was the wrong work for her, personally. She reset her expectations.

That's not to say she gave up her hopes for a promotion. In fact, they only intensified. But her strategy changed substantially. She redefined her role in the company, abandoning her career path in the operations organization and accepting a position in what many considered a less prestigious part of the business. There she could leverage many of her project leadership skills and open herself up to other opportunities. Today, she is thriving in her new role and taking her leadership potential to a new level. Her adaptive capacity enabled her to redirect herself toward what was most relevant for her personally, as opposed to what others expected. It took courage, but it also created the foundation for her to be a far more effective leader.

Open Up

A financially successful and powerful senior sales executive had achieved continual revenue growth and profitability for his regional business by deploying relatively similar strategic go-to-market and operational tactics for many years. In addition to not wanting to mess with success, many on his team were reluctant to suggest new approaches to the leader. They viewed him as cranky, headstrong, and resistant to new ideas.

Meanwhile, the firm's executive team, recognizing the need for a business transformation, had begun a series of executive assessments to evaluate and develop leaders who could take the company to the next level. As a part of the process, this executive was identified as someone with the potential to take on roles of increasing scope and importance. At the same time, the assessments yielded a very tough critique of his current leadership style and impact—feedback that was surprising to the leader, who had a very different impression of his performance in this area.

Many individuals, especially those who are accustomed to success, would have disregarded such discordant feedback and continued to go about "business as usual." After all, who could argue with his past track record?

But rather than shut down, the executive's competitive energy kicked in, in a positive way. He opened up to what he recognized as constructive criticism and engaged a professional coach to help him develop the more effective qualities of his innate leadership style, while quieting some of the practices that no longer served him, his team, or his company.

But it took more than this executive recognizing the need to change personally. He also had to overcome what was essentially a lack of faith among his team members that he could change. They had become so used to what they considered inflexibility that they would set him up, whether consciously or not, to fall back into his less productive leadership behaviors, almost in an attempt to prove that he'd not really changed. But to this executive's credit, he stayed on his evolutionary path. As a result, even during the economic downturn, his business showed growth, year after year. He not only reinvented his business, his organization, and his personal leadership style, he made life choices that have ultimately made him a happier person as well. His personal transformation also instilled a new rhythm and discipline to his own leadership team. Following his lead, they took a closer look at their own leadership styles. Since then, several members have been asked to take on larger, higher impact roles within the company.

It's Personal

I had a similar, personal experience. I was working hard, achieving my goals, and making an impression among the most senior leadership of the company. Then, one day, the news came: I had a recurrence of cancer. My body was telling me something that I otherwise refused to hear. I needed to stop and explore what that was. It is not uncommon for these kinds of physical wake-up calls to pave the way for personal and professional transformation. I asked myself, what do I want my life (and my legacy) to be? Take the time to ask yourself and visualize what it looks and feels like. If you only had five years to live, how would you want to live and what impact would you want to have? These are the most difficult questions, but they can bring a crispness and focus to life and your leadership platform. Take time to cleanse your priorities. There is nothing more powerful.

CHAPTER 3
Essential Traits 4-6

These essential traits continue to build off of traits 1-3, expanding the relationships between each trait.

Essential Trait 4:
An Experimental Mind

As you can tell, re-creation, while imperative, is not easy, and you don't always get it right the first time. That's okay. In fact, it is a defining characteristic of this next trait: the experimental mind. While more of an operations focus and engineering mentality may have been successful in the past, today's global leader needs to be more of an inventor and an experimenter, willing to try out a new idea (a hypothesis) and recognize that failure (disproving the hypothesis) can be just as valuable, if not more so, than when the hypothesis turns out to be correct. When you discover what doesn't work, you learn something, develop a new hypothesis, test it again, and eventually make a discovery that can benefit the business. Experimentation is a critical component of the reinvention process—whether you are reinventing a product, a solution, your business model or organizational structure, and even an industry platform or standard.

A spirit of inquiry that allows for continual learning is another of the five basic leadership qualities that Bennis and Thomas describe in *Geeks and Geezers*. The downfall for many leaders I have observed is that they reach a point where they stop learning. Once they have "made it" (an achievement level they often defined early in their careers—such as becoming a vice president of a division—when they and the world were very different), they become complacent to some degree. It's as if a switch turns off, and they are motivated differently. They are no longer thriving in settings where they are learning new and different ways of doing things. No longer are they pushing themselves out of their comfort zones to achieve a little bit more than they thought they could. No longer are they taking on those important career-building (and potentially career-limiting) assignments that define their leadership brand. Over time, there is a "settling in" that comes with the sense that they've arrived (even though what they have achieved is often tied to a goal they set much earlier in their career, and as such is probably not as relevant as it once was). With this comes a tendency to settle for the status quo, to make fewer important (and high risk) decisions, and, often as a result, underachieve in the face of transformation and change.

They become complacent at best, and overly protective at worst, of their coveted positions. Learning a new way of doing something, or worse yet, failing by doing something differently, could knock them from what they falsely consider a position of power and control. They mistakenly believe that from their advanced positions they should know all of the answers, whereas the experimentally minded leader knows it is actually about asking all the right questions, challenging assumptions, and learning from mistakes. As my colleague, Wim Elfrink, chief globalisation officer for Cisco describes it, "As leaders get older, they can become prisoners of their own experiences." If this happens, he says it is the "kiss of death" for the global leader. Unfortunately, this is the kind of thinking and behavior many business schools actually encourage, whether intentionally or not, when they emphasize management over experimentation, a topic we will explore further in chapter 6.

The good news is that experimentation is once again finding its place in large corporations. We are entering a new era of innovation according to Scott Anthony, managing partner of the innovation and growth consulting firm, Innosight. In his article, "The New Corporate Garage" (2012), Anthony describes how entrepreneurial individuals working in large organizations, often without direct reports or traditional areas of responsibility, are able to attract the right players and resources within the corporation and among its larger network to solve what are often significant global problems. The success of these corporate catalysts is dependent upon the company leaders being willing to decentralize certain innovative activities, while still keeping them central to the corporation's overall strategy, a topic we will discuss in more detail in chapter 5 on innovation.

For those who would challenge this approach, saying the world is moving too fast to take time to test, tweak, and test again, I would argue that the world is too complex and too unpredictable to do otherwise. The secret is to learn faster and change even faster than your competitors. It requires a unique combination of curiosity, perseverance, and the next essential trait: the freedom to fail, fast. Darwin had it right when he said: "It is not the strongest of the species that survives, nor the most intelligent, but the one most responsive to change."

Essential Trait 5:
Freedom to Fail, Fast

Many companies still see failure as far riskier and more painful than the success that can be achieved by playing it safe, and they set up their incentive plans to support the status quo, as opposed to innovation. As a result, many would-be corporate catalysts will be tempted to leave, taking their good ideas—and, more importantly, their passion to make them reality—to more hospitable environments. To attract and retain these all-important innovators, global leaders need to have a certain degree of comfort with failure and the ability to instill that sensibility within their organizations. That's not to say a leader wakes up on any given morning and says, "I want to go to work and fail today." No one does. But they recognize that failure is (and must be) part of the process of attaining success. Many of the leaders profiled in this book share a similar sentiment: They are willing to be fired for having the courage to do their jobs well, as opposed to keeping their jobs by playing it safe. Think back to the similar discussion about executives at the top who would rather play it safe. They have not mastered the art of failing fast.

I firmly believe that failure is a necessary ingredient to success. Leaders need to learn how to fail: How to understand it, learn from it, and most importantly, how to recover from it. Learning how to fail is essential if you want to know how to be successful. As Winston Churchill said, "Success is the ability to go from one failure to another with no loss of enthusiasm." For Amazon's Jeff Bezos, it's about having fun and loving invention. But he adds that it also comes with an understanding that "If you are going to invent, you need to be long-term thinking because invention takes time and not everything...will work out" (Lashinsky, 2012).

Failure is not the opposite of success but rather an integral part of the invention, reinvention, and innovation process. The Denver Art Museum recently had an exhibit focused on how Vincent Van Gogh became the truly exceptional artist he was, especially considering that he had no formal training. While the artwork on display was stellar, two quotes from the artist stood out, including one from early in his career when he was still learning how to draw and paint. In 1882, he wrote that, "Success is sometimes the outcome of a whole string of failures." Two years and many failures later, he remained committed to his path, writing "Onward—and it doesn't matter a damn if it fails; if it fails, do it again." Van Gogh did some amazing things in his life, including realizing that failure is not only an option—it is essential. A leader who can accept and learn from failure is going to be much more creative than one who avoids risk for fear that something could go wrong. In every place where one is setting out to do something on the edge, failure is likely. There will always be a hiccup, a glitch, a misunderstanding, or a product introduced to market too early (or worse yet, too late). Within each failure are lessons that develop experienced judgment to apply to subsequent reinvention or innovative projects.

A key element to learning how to fail is to understand how it affects you, personally. Over the years I have crafted many executive development plans where I recommended that a leader take a role in which he would likely fail. I have spent a great deal of time with the executives I have coached, exploring the messages about failure that they've learned (typically early in life). For many, the lessons learned are that they are less worthy, for others that they are less lovable.

For many of the more successful leaders, failure does not carry the neurotic stigma it does for others. They are able to recognize failure not as something that happens to or because of them, but rather as a normal and expected part of life. With this perspective, they grant themselves "permission to fail." Without the associated emotional baggage, they can more objectively deconstruct their failures, assess the various aspects, and learn from what happened.

Here's an example: I once worked with an executive who had moved around enough so that he was relatively comfortable starting work in a new company or position. He could usually assess the dynamics and make the necessary adjustments to his personal leadership style to succeed in the new work environment. But not so with his most recent move. He had entered the firm unprepared for what I call the corporate antibodies that were ready to attack him as a foreign substance. He tried the methods that he had used successfully in the past to win people over, but he did not get the traction he had experienced previously. In his midyear review, his boss told him he was failing and needed to turn things around in order to keep his job. Despite his unfamiliarity with this kind of predicament, the executive, to his credit, took an analytical approach. He not only considered carefully what his boss had said, he went out into the organization and gathered more feedback, recognizing it would not all be positive. He asked those he trusted, as well as those with whom he had been struggling. Then he objectively assessed what he heard—what he was doing right and wrong—and began to make the necessary adjustments to his style. Today, he is a role model for leadership in the same company. In more psychological terms, he was able to first normalize and then deconstruct his failure, both of which are required to learn from mistakes and move on.

Putting my full psychologist hat on for a minute, the clinical word for the extreme fear of failure is *atychiphobia*. It can create a paralyzing level of anxiety, in the face of real or imagined failure. In its most acute form, the person is so concerned about failing that he refuses to try any more. The response usually takes one of two forms: the individual either withdraws from any situation where failure is even a slight possibility, or tries to control the anxiety by falsely believing that perfection is attainable.

One of the higher potential leaders I have had the opportunity to coach struggled with a fear of failure. As a child, she was taught that failure is not acceptable. When she did make mistakes, she disappointed her father greatly, and he made her feel stupid (which she certainly wasn't) and unloved—feelings that only grew with each subsequent misstep. This executive carried her resulting anxiety around with her for years, forming what some call a "good girl" syndrome because she is always trying to please those around her.

She compensated by achieving small successes, rather than putting herself in situations where she could potentially have a tremendous impact but which also came with a high risk of failure. As part of her executive development plan, she was intentionally placed in a role where failure was inevitable. But despite what you might think, she was not being set up to fail. The organization made it clear that the intention was to help her succeed (in the long run), but that to do so, she would need to experience what it feels like to fail (in the short-term), and understand how those failures can position for success in the future. In other words, she needed to succeed at failing. I supported her as her executive coach through this process, helping her to explore how she reacted when she did fail, and what kinds of changes she could make to better face her fears.

To help her try out her new approach outside the work environment, she accepted a leadership seat on a small nonprofit board. She also collaborated with a professor at a local university to teach a class on a topic that she knew enough about, but on which she was not a noted expert. In addition to training herself to think differently about failure, she took on a new sport to literally build and use some new muscles. All of these were situations she would previously not have willingly entered. Over the course of her coaching, she worked through all of the neurotic beliefs about what it means to fail that she formed through her childhood. No one punished her. No one said she was stupid. No one sent her to the corporate penalty box for remediation. Most importantly, she learned that she would not only survive but could thrive in situations in which success wasn't necessarily predictable or assured, and even when it was not attainable.

As the Nobel Prize winner André Gide once said, "Man cannot discover new oceans unless he has the courage to lose sight of the shore." People who do extraordinary things have the confidence to take on massive amounts of risk. They are no less aware of the meaning of failure as I can tell, but they are much more comfortable with the concept.

A leader's job is not to accept failure, but rather to create the kind of environment, the culture if you will, where people are encouraged to question, test, and experiment; an environment that allows them to fail, albeit fast and productively. The most innovative companies fail fast and fail often. How the leader handles failure sets an example for the whole organization. Leaders who have mastered the art of failure talk openly and constructively about it. They characterize failure as part of the innovative process. They recognize that they might get it wrong, but they are okay with that dynamic, as awkward as it is, as long as it leads them closer to getting it right.

On the other hand, some failures are potentially fatal to a company, its brand, or its ability to deliver, and in the worst of cases, to the people who use its products. These types of failures must be avoided. For example, if you are a food or drug manufacturer you must do everything in your power and exert the control necessary to prevent contaminated products from making it to market.

When I talk about freedom to fail, I mean giving your organization permission to bet on projects that have a strong potential, but not a guarantee, for success. In doing so, one sets a tone that the organization embraces exploration, experimentation, and risk taking when and where it makes sense.

This is not unlike how healthy, mature parents are comfortable letting their children explore the world and learn from making mistakes. Yes, it is a parent's job and inclination to protect his child from serious harm, but it is also his responsibility to help prepare his child to lead a productive adult life. As a child psychologist, I used to tell parents that if their kids didn't have at least one Band-Aid on them, they weren't exploring their world enough. But you allow that exploration within some reasonable boundaries; you don't allow a three year-old to cross a busy street on her own. As an emerging leader, do you have at least one "Band-Aid" on? If not, are you pushing the boundaries as much as you could or should? We will explore more about raising the future global leaders in chapter 7.

Essential Trait 6:
Constuctive Collaboration

I've said it before, and I will say it again: Global leaders think big. In the context of this trait, they see themselves and their organizations as part of something much bigger, which correlates to having a strong sense of responsibility for the well-being of their companies and the larger ecosystem in which they exist.

In the early 1960s, Peter Drucker helped managerial science see corporations as social, not just industrial, systems. Today's global leaders go one step further, seeing corporations as if they are part of living systems, in which the success of the individual is dependent upon the success of the larger whole. In the business world, they understand that the success of the corporation is dependent upon the success of the broader ecosystems.

It's really no different from the adage: Don't compete for portions of the pie; grow the pie bigger. But for some reason, the value of collaboration, as opposed to unbridled competition, is still one that many business leaders struggle to embrace. The reason, says Amazon's Bezos, is that people often think about business like a sports competition, where at the end of the game, there is a clear winner and a clear loser. On the contrary, he says, "Typically in business, industries rise and fall, and there are multiple winners in most cases" (Rose, 2012). As an example, when asked about the current leaders in social media, he said it's not going to be Facebook or LinkedIn or Twitter that wins; it's all three. Their individual success will beget interest in each other, as well as in other new media, even those that have not yet been imagined. That doesn't mean competition is out. In fact, in many respects it is fiercer than ever before, but today's global leader needs to know when it makes sense to compete and when to collaborate. Global leaders need to be both dominant players in the market and trusted business partners, one of the many dichotomies they must understand and accept.

This is another example of why a strong sense of self and purpose is so important. There's no question, today's global leaders have to be formidable competitors, but the way they compete is often different. For Jeff Bezos, it's a matter of focus and priority. He says, "Some companies have more of a conqueror mentality; if you look at their strategic plan, it starts with the three top enemies they are going to crush this year." He says Amazon, on the other hand, stays focused on the customer over its competitors. That's not to say Amazon doesn't pay attention to the competition. "You don't want to live in a hermetically sealed bubble," says Bezos. "We want to know what other companies are doing...Is there somebody out there doing some element of what we do better than we do it and if so, how do we improve?" (Rose, 2012).

For Jim Whitehurst, CEO of Red Hat, improvement of his company's core product (Linux software) depends on cooperation among software developers around the world far beyond those on Red Hat's payroll. This approach is in sharp contrast to the more common economics of scarcity in which something of value is protected by copyrights and is only available to those willing to pay for it. In Whitehurst's world, value is actually created by maximizing access, which increases the size of the brain trust working on a given problem. This approach, long lauded by the free software movement, can yield unprecedented results.

While just one of a growing number of examples, consider the case of some gamers who, in just 10 days, were able to unlock the code to an enzyme that could hold the secrets to the cure for AIDS, something scientists at the University of Washington had been trying, unsuccessfully, to do for 10 years. The gamers in question were playing *FoldIt*, an online game that enables players from around the world to talk to one another and collaborate on problems related to the structure of proteins (Puiu 2011).

Red Hat, meanwhile, has turned this approach into a profitable business model. Whitehurst admits that to be successful, he had to suspend traditional value judgments about sharing and embrace the concept that collaboration can lead to a better product—in his case, better software—at significantly lower development costs. But it's not enough for just the leader to believe. Your community has to share that same belief, that there is something in it for them as well. This is not unlike how Apple was able to attract a bevy of developers to create applications for the iPhone. As a result, Apple found value in a more successful product; developers found value through a platform for their creations; and consumers enjoyed the value of a new smartphone with unheard of capabilities.

So constructive collaboration requires that team members are able to suspend their own judgments about which approach is best, and even more importantly, their need to be right. The right attitude is essential, but so is process. An inventor by nature, Jeff Bezos says his favorite activity is brainstorming. To overcome the natural tendency for people to come up with myriad reasons why a new idea won't work, Bezos sets up a process by which his teams get to spend an agreed upon amount of time picking new ideas apart, after which they have to force rank each of the barriers and then make a concerted effort to find solutions for each one.

For global executives leading organizations across multiple cultures, constructive collaboration is not about forcing values on others, nor is it about giving up their own. It's a delicate balance that necessitates openness, curiosity, and empathy to the experiences of others. It starts with understanding why people behave the way they behave.

Let me give you an example. I was delivering a keynote address on global leadership, during which a woman in the audience asked me about a situation in which a businesswoman had wanted to go out to dinner in Saudi Arabia with her male colleagues. Her request was denied, on the grounds that it was against the law and the woman could be arrested. The questioner wanted my opinion on the role corporations should play in bolstering women's rights in the Middle East. The question made me think. On one hand, as a fairly evolved Western woman, I wanted to say that corporations should demand equality for employees regardless of gender. But the social anthropologist in me took a different approach. I responded by asking the woman, and the audience, to consider the context and the assumptions we hold. As Westerners, do we assume when a woman is denied the right to dine with her colleagues that she is being oppressed? Or have we considered the long-standing social and religious history and culture of the Middle East? Are there other measures to determine if a woman is being treated fairly? Are there ways to ensure her equality and standing in the workplace, if not society in general?

As we explored the topic further, the woman took pause, recognizing that her perspectives were coming from a Western ethos and that a solution needed to take into consideration the cultural dynamics of the region. Her bias was driving her desire to take a specific approach, not necessarily what would be most effective under the circumstances. Was she trying to do the right thing? Of course! Was she looking at the issue in an open and culturally sensitive manner? Not so much.

This is one of the hardest areas for global leaders. For most of us, our sense of what's right and wrong, good and bad, is defined very early in life, typically adopted from the values of our primary caregivers and from the places where we were raised. The stronger your sense of self, the stronger you hold to your values. The challenge is in the difference between moral values and cultural values, and understanding which you consider absolute and which need to be seen in the context of the part of the world in which you are operating. How do you justify the differences? Can you or should you? And how do you reconcile the world in which you are operating versus cultural values, while holding true to your immutable values in a world where people think, act, and believe differently from you? This can be even more challenging for executives who are accustomed to being in control. Not only do they need to exert less of a heavy hand within their organizations, but they also need to be comfortable with the dynamics of interdependent relationships with organizations and individuals that are outside their official span of control. After all, they are not the boss of the whole world, and even if they were, being boss does not mean you can or should make the rules. We will explore this further in the next essential trait: balance between control and chaos.

To get to this level of comfort, global leaders need to be particularly adept at identifying who can be trusted and at gaining the trust and respect of critical players within the ecosystem. Once again, a strong sense of self plays a critical role. The better you understand yourself, the better attuned you will be to others and whether they make good partners. Meanwhile, your sense of self drives authenticity (another essential trait I will address later), which makes it easier for others to be willing to trust you. I am not saying this takes the place of solid due diligence. But trust is being recognized as a critical and quantifiable factor in business success. In his book, *The Speed of Trust*, Stephen M.R. Covey, son of noted business consultant Dr. Stephen R. Covey, says trust can be measured in terms of time and productivity. For example, it changes how fast you are able to make a decision and keep from second guessing yourself or others, as well as the ability to create and to learn from others. In a global business environment, trust is even more important, says Covey. In an interview on CNN, Covey explained: "You overcome [cultural differences]...through how you behave. You behave in a way that respects the differences and that actually listens first and tries to understand first" (2010).

CHAPTER 4

Essential Traits 7-10

Essential Traits 7-10 round out the essential traits, which we will explore more deeply in the later sections of the book.

Essential Trait 7:
Balance Between Control and Chaos

The ability to know what still works, what doesn't, and what needs to be reworked—as defined in Essential Trait #4: The Experimental Mind—plays into the next trait, which is finding that right balance between control and chaos. While businesses must continually evolve and innovate to stay relevant, their leaders still need to manage people and maintain operational excellence to ensure profitability. Often that requires a leader to build the right balance within the leadership team. Remember Essential Trait #3 and the courage to re-create your team? Even a company as "cool" as Facebook needed someone like Sheryl Sandberg to figure out how to make a profit. Facebook founder Mark Zuckerberg acknowledged this in a comment he made to *The New Yorker* about hiring Sandberg as chief operating officer: "There are people who are really good managers, people who can manage a big organization...And then there are people who are very analytical or focused on strategy. Those two types don't usually tend to be in the same person. I would put myself much more in the latter camp."

With the right team, leaders can exert some control at the core of their organizations to ensure optimal performance, while letting the reins loose on the edge where the true innovation happens and where too much control can stifle creativity. Today's global leaders need to not only learn to live with, but also to appreciate, messiness on the outer edge of their organizations, a topic explored in more detail in chapter 5 on innovation.

This requires coexisting in two worlds, one that is more reminiscent of the past, where a certain level of control and oversight is important to drive today's performance expectations, and another where the leader sets the vision and then gives permission to those working on the edge to self-organize and find solutions—often to problems that have not even been considered or that do not exist yet.

John Chambers at Cisco Systems recognized the need to set the vision and then let go. He established the strategic objectives for innovation at the company: the creation of new products, services, and customer solutions to meet the needs of a changing, emerging, and diverse marketplace, and then he let his chief innovation officer Marthin DeBeer run with them. Marthin was charged with building the innovation organization, the Emerging Technologies Group (ETG). While the core business stayed focused on growth of traditional product offerings—routers and switches—Marthin was freed up to explore new business and market opportunities. In this regard, Marthin (under Chambers' leadership) was a forebearer of the "new corporate garage" phenomenon discussed earlier. ETG served as an incubation center where innovative ideas could be developed, tested, and ultimately translated into business opportunities. And under Marthin's leadership, ETG launched some of Cisco's highest profile (and most disruptive) technology projects.

Why were Marthin and his ETG team so important to Cisco's ability to balance control and chaos? Because Marthin and his elite team of innovators were able to operate outside many of the rules that governed the core business. This gave them the freedom to build new technologies that would serve Cisco in the future. Marthin hired entrepreneurs who were rebels by nature. He and the ETG team then set up several crowdsourcing processes to gather intelligence from both within the company and from the larger market. And they set up disciplined innovation funnels that further pressure-tested the viability of ideas. Plus, he co-developed a "corporate garage" process by which these viable ideas would be further tested and developed by emerging business leaders. We talk about one of those processes—the action learning forums—in the best practices section in chapter 6.

ETG represented a cultural shift for Cisco. While this group adopted many of Cisco's cultural and operating values, they also created their own operating principles that were unique, by necessity, to an organization that would need to live in the chaos of innovation, transformation, and disruptive change. This group stood for creativity, disruption, risk taking, experimentation, and rapid change.

Global leaders also need to be comfortable in an environment where success—and the multiple paths to get there—is not clearly defined. They need to be comfortable in the driver's seat of the car with their foot on the gas, while they rebuild the engine if not redesign the entire car, the highway they are driving on, and even what their final destination looks like. This is vastly different from a world in which change occurred more slowly and in an incremental and linear manner (with greater predictability), and when business transformation was easier to plan, control, and measure. A

CEO could demand improved performance through increased efficiency and productivity, and managers could engage business process improvement or supply chain management initiatives to meet those demands. Not only did they know what needed to be done, they knew what to measure and how. Did they produce more with fewer resources? Did they reduce transportation costs? Were customer service levels improved?

Measuring success on the "edge" is much harder. There are very few key performance indicators for the process of essentially creating something that does not yet exist, something we discuss further in chapter 5. Measuring the results also typically requires much longer time frames than most executives, companies, boards of directors, or financial markets have the patience to accommodate. The danger for many companies is that the core business will want to utilize metrics that they have deployed historically, as opposed to those that are relevant for an evolving future. Further, when it comes to investing in innovation, many executives and their boards are reluctant to divert resources from what they consider "sure bets"—what has worked in the past—to fund something that may or may not generate a return on that investment. This dynamic gets a lot of companies in trouble, when they let past performance rule over future needs.

By understanding and balancing the needs of both worlds, leaders can help their organizations stay profitable today, which can help financially support innovation for the future. To do so, leaders need to be comfortable with the messiness inherent in a knowledge (versus industrial) economy. Innovation is ripe with opportunities for incredible breakthrough successes (like Google), and it is fraught with risk. Even when innovation works, the task of bringing a new product or service into the core of the business is also messy. To do messy well, you must be able to abandon your need for prediction and control and adopt a level of comfort with ambiguity. And to deal with ambiguity, you must be a bit ambivalent yourself. It's about both/and, not either-or.

This is an important development hurdle to overcome; in fact, the most successful global leaders are those who thrive in situations that are ambiguous by nature. On the other hand, leaders who get stuck in either-or (as compared to the multimodal thinker's ability to hold seemingly disparate ideas) have a hard time dealing with uncertainty. They want to control the outcome, but that's impossible when you are trying to create something completely new or different. For some executives, the need for precision and predictability is too strong to let the messy emerge. If you are a leader who demands precision, ask yourself why. What purpose does it serve? It is an illusion that precision, or perfection, is attainable, or that you are ever, fully, in control. There is no right answer; there are just some answers that are better than others. If you are uncomfortable making mistakes, you will be too uncomfortable to succeed in the long run. You must learn not only to live with the tension, but also to thrive in it. And you must help others on your team become more comfortable with ambiguity as well. If not, you and your company will get stuck, while those who don't mind getting a little dirty are out building a better world.

Essential Trait 8:
Global Change Agent
(The Soul of Leadership)

The most successful leaders embody a sense of greatness, but not in an egotistical way, more as a matter of fact. They believe they were put on this world for a greater purpose—to make the world a better place—and that larger sense of self drives much of what they do. For example, consider Oprah Winfrey. She used her confidence and ambition to turn what began as a mission to expand the world of stay-at-home moms into a multibillion dollar empire. At approximately the same time, British businesswoman Anita Roddick was founding The Body Shop on a pledge not to sell any products tested on animals. The cosmetic manufacturer and retailer was one of the first companies to promote fair trade with third world countries. Along the way, Roddick helped shape the ethical consumerism market, before selling her company for more than $1 billion in 2006.

Other global leaders expand their platforms to become catalysts for political, social, economic, and environmental change. Infosys' Nandan Nilekani was recently recruited by Indian Prime Minister Manmohan Singh to head a project that will create national identification cards for the people in the country. A unique 12-digit number will be issued to each resident of India, stored in a centralized database, and linked to basic demographics and biometric information (similar to a social security number in the U.S.). This will prove extremely valuable to the world's second most populous nation, as it will allow better census activity and bring resources to where they are most needed.

Drawing again on the theory of living systems, insightful global leaders recognize that unbridled competition for limited resources can create scarcity to a degree that threatens not only individual organizations but also the much broader environment in which they operate. Leadership at a global level has a tremendous capacity to change the world, for good or for ill. Unlike industrial-age thinking that at times disregarded or diminished the importance of environmental and social responsibility, global leaders today are more aware of the impact their operations have and are adjusting processes and policies to promote sustainability. In fact, many of the executives interviewed for this book commented that growth going forward must depend upon business models that support sustainability: of communities, of workforces, of the environment.

For many global leaders, making the world a better place is not just a business necessity; it can also create market opportunities. Once again, it requires a longer-term perspective, but it can pay dividends over time. Take GE and IBM as examples. GE began making investments in China years ago, in order to demonstrate commitment to the Chinese government and to the people of the region. When the sleeping giant was ready to return to prominence on the world stage, GE had already paid the price of admission and secured choice seats, while many companies eager to reach the world's largest audience scrambled to pay scalper's prices to get in the door. But for GE, this is not a short-term commitment. Recently, GE invested more than two billion dollars to boost research and development in China and fund new local joint ventures in areas such as technology and financial services. And the rewards keep coming, with the company signing four new joint venture agreements with Chinese state-owned firms in the energy and railway industries.

Over the past 30 years, IBM has been busy establishing more than 30 branch offices across China, extending the company's software, hardware, and service presence into 320 cities. But this is not just about business growth. IBM is uniquely positioned to provide solutions that help the government advance its agenda: to build a more harmonious society and improve the way the government and businesses collaborate. Yes, it took a big investment and it took patience, but today both of those companies have access and positions that other companies envy. Sometimes it takes a big investment—other times a big idea. Sometimes the benefits are indirect, such as increased access or better working relationships; other times, you can make money just by doing good. Take a couple of the examples highlighted in Scott Anthony's article, "The New Corporate Garage."

Unilever set out to solve a significant global problem, especially in developing countries: lack of access to safe drinking water. It took a group of 100 company scientists collaborating around the world, but Unilever was able to create a portable system that could provide safe drinking water, not only reliably but at a fraction of the cost of other high quality solutions. With strong sales and a significant unmet need still to be satisfied, Unilever has a multibillion dollar business in the making.

The agribusiness giant Syngenta set its sights on helping to cure world hunger by increasing the productivity of hundreds of millions of small farms around the world. By using sachets (the kind used for single dose product samples) the company could distribute the same crop protection chemicals used by large farms in much smaller, more affordable, and easier to use packaging suitable for small farms. The new distribution system, combined with a complementary education and training program, has led to multimillion dollar sales in Kenya alone, with plans to expand the program in other countries in Africa and Asia (Anthony, 2012).

What makes some leaders take a chance on these more altruistic and unproven ventures? The psychological dynamic at play here is productive narcissism. I know, talking about the greater good and narcissism in the same sentence might not make sense at first. But let me explain the psychology behind this statement. Everyone is born narcissistic; it's a survival skill, but there is a continuum, ranging from unproductive (unhealthy) to productive (healthy) narcissism. Those leaders and companies higher on the maturity curve are best positioned to take advantage of these greater good business opportunities. In fact, they may be the only ones to even recognize their existence or potential.

So what about narcissism? As I said, we are all narcissistic to some degree. As a very young child—say one to three years old— it's very normal to be narcissistic. At that age, the answers to all of a child's questions are very self-centric: Why is the sky blue? Because it is my favorite color! Why does the sun shine? Because I am cold! But as a child grows up and begins to have a better understanding of his relationship to the world, narcissism can manifest differently. For example, when a child inevitably does something wrong, if the parent helps him understand that it was his actions and not him as an individual that was wrong, the child can grow up with what the textbooks call primary narcissism or healthy self love. In this way, children are taught at an early age to learn from their mistakes (Think back to Essential Trait #4: The Experimental Mind and #5: Freedom to Fail, Fast). It's this kind of narcissism that can later inspire innovative leaders like Yuri Jain at Unilever or Nick Musyoka at Syngenta to come up with completely new approaches to some of the world's most complex and monumental problems. In his book *All About Me*, Simon Crompton describes the healthy narcissist as "someone who has a real sense of self-esteem that can enable them to leave their imprint on the world, but who can also share in the emotional life of others" (2008). Crompton also references the work of psychoanalyst and anthropologist Michael Maccoby who claims, "The natural energy and individuality of narcissists is the key to much industrial progress and innovation" (2003).

On the other hand, the inability of a child to distinguish between being a good or bad person and doing good or bad things lays the groundwork for unproductive narcissism. Over time, individuals who are not able to recover from the various bruises to the ego that we all suffer may develop unhealthy narcissistic characteristics. Rather than having a healthy sense of confidence that matches reality, unhealthy narcissists assume grandiose demeanors, lauding their power and greatness over others. Pay attention to the man behind the curtain in the *Wizard of Oz* and how his lack of self-esteem manifested as a domineering and frightening wizard. The leaders profiled in this book are all productive narcissists who are using their global leadership positions to set the bar for a new code of ethics for how business should be done in the world. They know they are special, but they use that confidence to help raise others up, not to denigrate them.

Healthy or productive narcissism is also related to several of the other essential traits, as it supports a strong sense of self, adaptability, a natural curiosity, and an ability to live well with others. The productive narcissist is open to creating a team that challenges her, while the unproductive narcissist tends to create a human buffer made up of "yes" people. This just perpetuates the problem. Think of celebrities who have been in trouble, again and again. Oftentimes, when a celebrity first acts poorly, a handler will protect him from the consequences. Then, if the wrongdoings escalate, and someone on the team questions the celebrity's action, the celebrity may bring in a new team. This new team will continue to provide protection (or more accurately insulation) until the wrongdoings become so egregious that higher powers take over and the celebrity lands in jail or rehabilitation.

Narcissism follows another continuum, this time of insight-fulness. Those in the unproductive range have little to no insight as to how they show up in the world and are often blind to opportunities for growth. It's hard to change if you don't begin with a sense of who you are. Admittedly, it's difficult to change this pattern in adults, although I have seen change happen in individuals who have particularly strong moral characters. Unfortunately, the lessons learned from being insightful are just too painful for someone with low self-esteem and ultimately may reinforce the unhealthy narcissistic tendencies.

Insight—whether in a leader or in a corporation—also determines the potential to recognize the value of being a good corporate citizen. Some of the literature speaks to what is called corporate narcissism, which in its unproductive manifestation is characterized by a singular focus on profits. While this can achieve benefits in the short run, it can limit an organization's ability to recognize what's most important for long-term success. It can also be demoralizing to employees who are driven not just by their financial compensation, but also by the desire to make a difference.

Essential Trait 9:
Empathy as a Business Imperative

The level of insight that a global leader possesses is closely correlated to the next trait: empathy and respect for the human element. For many businesspeople, a word like empathy seems too soft for the fiercely competitive, results-driven world in which they live. But empathy can yield some very tangible business results on many fronts, from employee engagement to product design to identifying new market opportunities. The clinical definition of empathy is: "the capacity to know emotionally what another is experiencing

77

from within the frame of reference of that other person" (Berger, 1987). I know, still sounds soft, just maybe a little more, well, clinical. But let's explore what the capability to understand "what another is experiencing" and "within the frame of reference" can do for the global business leader.

Let's start with the leader of a business that sells products or services to widely diverse markets around the globe. For her company, a product that is a top seller in one market might not work at all in another. Kodak missed this fact with its first point-and-shoot camera. It decided to manufacture the product in Brazil, because at the time, products sold in that highly populated and emerging market had to be produced in the country. That part made sense. Where the now-bankrupt film and camera maker made its mistake was thinking that the product it manufactured for the Brazilian market—which required a lower price point—would also do well with American consumers. To Americans, the product appeared to be lower quality than its competitors, an impression that Kodak was never able to overcome, even with later models. Understanding the needs of the market you are trying to serve is critical. In contrast, companies that recognize the value of under-standing their customers and the world they live in—their frame of reference if you will—are able to create more relevant versions of their products for specific markets. Think back to our discussion in chapter 1 about Reliance's ability to capture the mobile phone market in India by creating a much more affordable model with features customized to the needs of rural populations and localized languages. If you don't have empathy, if you can't see beyond your own view of the world or your own assumptions about how things should or must be, it will be very hard to capitalize on these oppor-tunities. We will explore this topic further in the next chapter.

Until we can teach a computer to feel (and some would argue we will), the ability to empathize with the marketplace is an advantage that humans have over technology, even though technology still ranks as the number one driver for innovation among CEOs responding to the Conference Board CEO Challenge 2013. More telling from the report is that "six of the top 10 global strategies to support innovation are related to human capital" (Mitchell, Ray, and van Ark, 2012), which by the way was ranked as the number one challenge for leaders globally. This is something the world's leading design thinkers have known all along. They believe the nature of innovation itself is changing, being driven more by creativity than by high science. Just ask IDEO founder David Kelly. While his company is perhaps best known for designing the iconic mouse for the Mac computer—a design that is still used in virtually all mechanical mice today—IDEO today designs every-thing from cooktops to how a woman experiences a mammography appointment. The firm's approach, as described on the website, sounds a bit mysterious: "We identify new ways to serve and support people by uncovering latent needs, behaviors, and desires." But to hear Kelly describe it on a recent edition of *60 Minutes*, it's relatively straightforward. He says they watch the consumer (in his example, using a piece of software). "If he grimaces, we ask what point in the software he was at, and then we fix whatever the problem is." That's empathy in action.

Now, just imagine the power of an empathetic leader who is also a multimodal thinker. A leader with both of these essential traits not only knows what needs to be done (almost instinctively), but also knows how to orchestrate myriad players to bring that vision to life. The value of empathy extends beyond just customers, to how leaders motivate and engage with employees around the world and those who are part of their broader ecosystem.

Maya Strelar-Migotti, leader of Ericsson's IP/Broadband Business and one of the executives profiled in this book, has responsibility for an organization of 6,000 people in 18 different locations around the globe. She comes from a diverse background herself; born in Croatia, she has lived in Australia, Spain, Sweden, and now the United States. Maya says trust is critical to get everyone on her team speaking the same language, working toward the same goal. And communication underlies that trust. Maya says people want to understand the purpose behind their work: why the company is doing what it is doing and where it is going. A highly results-oriented, metrics-driven executive, she says companies often put too little emphasis on the softer side of the business: the people and the culture. That, Maya believes, is a mistake.

Essential Trait 10: Authenticity

The final essential trait, the one that ties it all together, is authenticity. I began with a strong sense of self, which as we have seen, supports many of the other traits. Unfortunately, many executives try to be something they are not, either because some overzealous public relations practitioners have crafted images they prefer or because the executives themselves think that once they have made it to the top they need to act like a CEO, whatever that means. Don't confuse this with my admonition that what worked in the past won't work going forward. What I am talking about here is who an executive is at the very core. You can learn to see the world differently, you can structure your company differently, you can even learn to think differently, but don't show up as someone you are fundamentally not.

Living in a manner that is shaped by what the world expects, versus who you are, will prove to be imprudent. Over the years, I have seen what can only be called the evolution of the empty or rehearsed executive, one who is so branded and controlled that he risks losing sight of who he is. At a minimum, it can shut down creativity, in much the same way that over-control can kill innovation in an organization. Once again, a strong sense of self can help an executive rise above who or what others want him to be.

I worked with an executive once who lived the life of rehearsed authenticity. He had many handlers who would craft his messages to make sure they were perfectly scripted and on point. But that same executive also had to have an equal number of handlers who would clean up after him when he chose to speak his mind. He never fully internalized the messages that were written for him, because they were not his. They were what others thought his constituents needed or wanted to hear. When he was on point, he came across as disingenuous. And when he was off point, he made people wonder who the real executive was, and what the real story was. Trust eroded, and as we discussed earlier, in a much bigger world, with larger ecosystems upon which your company depends, trust is a key success factor.

Authenticity is even more critical in a world of social networking, where anything you do or say can be captured and shared with the rest of connected humanity in a matter of minutes, if not seconds. I was reminded of this by a good friend the other day, who, when I told her I was taking my son to a karaoke birthday party, cautioned me not to get behind the microphone. Regardless of whether I can or cannot sing, the lesson to remember is that even something you do with the best of intentions in public can be taken out of context and used against you. Just ask anyone who has run for political office recently.

For Frits van Paasschen, CEO of Starwood Properties and one of the executives profiled later in this book, transparency is a fact of life. In his "manifesto" on leadership, written in early 2012 for the employees of his worldwide hotel and resort network, Frits says, "It is not enough to have a strong brand or a great product. People expect to know about the company behind the brand and the people behind the product. Thanks to Facebook, Wikileaks, and LinkedIn—there are virtually no degrees of separation anymore. All the world's a digital stage."

ESSENTIAL TRAITS AS A RECIPE FOR SUCCESS

As you read the executive profiles in section IV of the book, you will see many of these essential traits in action. Each of the executives exhibit certain traits (or combinations thereof) more than others, sometimes as a function of what a specific circumstance or objective requires, and other times as a reflection of his essential nature. One they all have in common is the first trait we discussed: a strong sense of self. I don't believe you have to excel at all of the essential traits to be a good leader. Take multimodal thinking—that trait in particular I believe is hardwired—you either have it, albeit to varying degrees, or you don't. But understanding who you are as an individual is essential; you identify your relative strengths and weaknesses and, as a leader, you ensure your leadership team has a full collection of the essential traits, to complement you, your organization, and the market you serve.

SECTION 3
Actions

CHAPTER 5

Innovation Unleashed: A Leadership Imperative

Most people are born creative. Unfortunately, creativity often decreases with age. Studies show that 98 percent of 5 year-olds test as "highly creative," compared to 2 percent of adults (Shapiro, 2008). Other research shows that at age 5, children use about 80 percent of their creative potential (they are essentially innovating every day), while that number drops to 2 percent by age 12 and stays there for most adults for the rest of their lives (Creating Minds. org, 2010).

But it doesn't have to be that way. I believe that by understanding what stifles creativity, we can help preserve our ability to innovate, as individuals and as organizations. And I would argue it's an imperative if we are to meet many of the challenges facing us on a global basis, from a lack of safe drinking water to global warming, let alone to keep our businesses competitive. Today's corporate leaders agree. A 2010 IBM poll of 1,500 CEOs identified creativity as the number one "leadership competency" of the future (Bronson and Merryman, 2010).

So what's the problem? My good friend and colleague Tony Wagner has written about these issues in two of his books, *Creating Innovators* and *The Global Achievement Gap*. He says one of the biggest impediments to creativity and innovation is the process of socialization, whether it is through parenting, our educational systems, organized sports, or bureaucratic corporate structures. Over time, we are taught to suppress our creative and curious impulses—worse yet, we become embarrassed by them and self-censor our ideas and thoughts—as we attempt to accommodate a world that has traditionally valued logic and analytical reasoning over curious exploration.

The solution (or at least one of them) is to think more like a child. I am constantly amazed by the incredibly insightful questions that my son Tucker asks, the imaginative stories that he makes up, the fabulous pictures that he sees in the clouds or paints on blank canvasses, and the passion he exudes when coming up with some inventive solution to a common everyday problem. It's exactly the way business leaders—and their teams—need to think.

One sunny afternoon, Tucker and I were taking a long nature walk. He decided that on this particular walk, we were going to do nothing but come up with new ideas. Earlier in the day, Tucker had told me he wanted a pet hamster, so I tasked him with coming up with a plan for how he would take care of his new pet. He wasted no time in telling me I was thinking too narrowly—by focusing on a plan—and that instead, we should think more broadly, about creating a hamster adventure. Over the next two hours, with over-the-top enthusiasm, Tucker engaged me in a discussion about a new business opportunity: an adopt-a-hamster website for children who aren't allowed to have hamsters of their own (or at least not until they produce a plan for their mothers). The site could post pictures, offer care and feeding suggestions, and have games where children could earn points for taking good care of their virtual hamsters. By the end of the walk, Tucker had devised something much greater than either of us had imagined at the onset. He even had some of my friends who hold executive roles in other companies in mind for positions such as CFO and head of sales and marketing for his new venture. For this creative and entrepreneurial 9 year-old, there is no fear of the unknown, of being judged, of taking risks, or of losing control, as is too often the case with adults in business.

As Tony Wagner has also stated, the world no longer cares about what you know, but rather what you do with what you know, and even more importantly, with what you don't know. Knowledge, today, is an essentially free commodity for most people. If you don't know something, you can Google a question and have an answer (or choice of answers) in seconds. What's important is how you take that newfound knowledge, or even the question, and turn it into something new, something innovative, something of value. The capability to bring innovative ideas successfully to market will be the determinant of global competitiveness of businesses, even nations, over the coming decade; innovative activity is one of the main drivers of business growth and economic progress.

Unfortunately, as Tony has learned through his research, our educational system is often radically at odds with what it takes to innovate. Traditional education promotes risk avoidance; students learn how *not to fail* by figuring out what teachers expect and how to deliver against that set of expectations. As a result, you are taught to think within narrow boundaries. Contrast that with the kind of environment or culture that produces innovators, where people are encouraged to try new things, to fail early, often, and fast. Innovation doesn't happen without trial and error, without research and development, because it is all about making mistakes and then learning from those mistakes. It is the process of picking oneself up, dusting oneself off, and moving forward that makes you stronger and willing to try, try again. It's also about the ability to keep trying even after you have found a solution, asking yourself, "Is there a better way?," which can be key to creating an environment of continual versus occasional innovation.

Interestingly, the process of design thinking—which historically has been only narrowly applied to create new products or new designs for existing products—is being applied more broadly in ways that can help leaders and corporations break free from their overly analytical approaches to thinking. As we have discussed, the engineering mind works well in economic models that rely on scaled efficiency, but not for those that demand solutions to meet the needs of diverse cultures and evolving markets. Design thinking takes into account information about people and cultures, overlays it with empathy about their experiences and needs, and translates that into new products and services, and often new ways of delivering solutions to the market. As Bruce Nussbaum, the former assistant managing editor in charge of *BusinessWeek's* innovation and design coverage, explains it: "Design thinking can be our guide to deep consumer understanding, visualization of possibilities, generative option-making, and strategic brand finding" (Nussbaum, 2009).

I recently attended Stanford's Hasso Plattner Institute of Design, or "d.school" as most call it. Originally started by IDEO founder David Kelly in a small trailer on the outskirts of Stanford University, today d.school occupies some of the most prestigious real estate in the center of the campus, with each course receiving twice as many applications as it has space for students. But while the d.school has moved onto the main campus, it is anything but a traditional learning environment. Everything is intended to get students out of their comfort zone. The building itself is more like a garage than a classroom, with a large mechanical door, concrete floors, and modular walls. The d.school's mission is to help students (mostly from higher education and the corporate world) rediscover their creative confidence. In addition to fostering their innate ability to come up with new ideas, the program helps them muster the courage to try them out in the real world. The brilliance of the program is its ability to apply (design) structure to something that by its very nature is chaotic.

While the d.school values innovation, it prioritizes the innovator. This makes complete sense in a world where innovation will be less dependent upon new technological advances and more on people working together to find new ways to apply what already exists, be it technology or processes, to new problems. Another differentiator is the program's interdisciplinary approach. The d.school is based on the belief that a diversity of backgrounds and perspectives opens the mind to new ideas, or encourages people to keep thinking of alternative solutions even after they have seemingly solved the problem.

Innovation consultant Stephen Shapiro agrees. In a speech available on his website, he tells a group of aerospace engineers that if 100 of them were working on a problem, adding one more engineer would probably not make much of a difference. But add a biologist, a nanotechnologist, even an artist or musician, and he says they might see the problem (and find the solution) through different eyes. Sometimes the breakthrough comes by embracing, rather than fighting, those moments of tension when there are differing opinions and approaches to problem solving. Sometimes it is as simple as asking yourself: Has someone else, someone from another discipline, solved a similar problem? That approach worked for one of Shapiro's clients—an office supply company trying to get customers to return and refill ink toner cartridges. The answer came when they considered how Netflix had solved a similar problem: getting customers to return their DVDs (2013).

Taking a more human-centric approach, d.school creates an "all in" experience in which students are encouraged to fully immerse themselves in the problems they are trying to solve. For many of these students, getting out of their usual environment can also help them get out of their overly analytical mindsets. Take for example the successful approach of one group of students when they took on the challenge of helping premature babies who were found to be more at risk of death or developing lifelong health problems in certain parts of the globe. The students flew to those regions to witness the situation firsthand. What they discovered was that the more traditional solution to the problem—providing incubators—would not be effective because these regions had limited, and often inconsistent, power sources. What they created was a low-cost infant warmer that can function without a continuous supply of electricity. They took an existing concept, a sleeping bag, and added an existing substance, a phase change material that is capable of storing and releasing large amounts of energy. The combination resulted in an infant warmer that can stay at a constant temperature for up to 6 hours without electricity. Their newly designed product is not only saving the lives of premature babies, it's also become a viable enterprise. The team created a charitable organization called Global Embrace, secured a contract with GE Healthcare and, through active partnerships with nongovernment organizations, is making its product available to qualifying hospitals and clinics in India, Somalia, and China.

The d.school teaches that innovation begins by understanding the essential needs of specific geographic, demographic, or psychographic markets. By honing their observation skills, and then drawing upon their collective ability to recognize patterns—to connect the dots if you will—d.school teams are much more adept at delivering what the customer wants than those who rely on more traditional approaches to customer research. In many companies, new products are still developed by talking to the customer and then building to what they say they want. As Marthin DeBeer explains it, if you want to build a new product for, say, the Brazilian market, you have to spend time there, to understand how people think and what they need. In his words, "you cannot read it in a whitepaper."

Product innovation superstars, like Procter & Gamble (P&G), rely more on ethnography, which seeks to understand why various cultures behave the way they do. In a sense, it is more about anthropology than it is about market research. By observing behaviors and understanding the meanings behind them, ethnographers can invent new products and services that change how people behave, not just what people buy. That's essentially what Google did first for researchers and more recently for those navigating from one location to another.

This ability to observe, understand, and innovate is still something that humans do better than computers. There is still a tremendous opportunity to accelerate and improve decision making, even achieve new realizations, using advanced computing capabilities such as IBM's Watson. But we should never discount the human element, especially en masse. In chapter 3, I mentioned how people playing *FoldIt*, a video game in which players try to fold proteins into the most stable configurations, were able to solve an HIV-related puzzle in a matter of weeks, something scientists had not accomplished in a decade of work. Now consider the collective success of people playing *eteRNA*, the next generation video game created by Adrian Treuille, the same computer scientist behind *FoldIt*. *EteRNA* was designed to solve a similar visual folding puzzle, this time related to RNA, the long-chained biological molecule that helps create the genetic code for some viruses. But unlike *FoldIt*, *eteRNA* asked gamers to submit their configurations, which scientists then used to create RNA in the lab. At first, the scientists thought the effort was a failure. Even though thousands of people played, none of the synthesized molecules folded into stable shapes. What the scientists failed to appreciate was the power of the community. When the gamers saw the results, they began analyzing their mistakes as a community and revising their strategies. Six months later, the players had learned how to fold RNA in a manner that could be successfully replicated in the lab.

The important point of this story is the human factor. People working together on this problem were better able to visualize the solution than any of the computers tasked with the same challenge. Treuille explained on the PBS television program "NovaScience" that you don't always know when you hire someone if that person will be good at the job. In this case, he says, "We sort of hired the world and the world turned out to be awesome" (2012). He envisions science—and I would expand that to include business innovation—as a team sport, not one with 30 people on a team, but more like 30 thousand. This point further illustrates the importance of Essential Trait #6: Constructive Collaboration. As leaders seek to increase innovation in their organizations, they should consider how they can harness the collective brainpower of their worldwide workforce, their customer base, and sometimes even the broader ecosystem in which they operate.

Beyond a willingness to think differently and together, innovation is enhanced by a deep-rooted desire (or as Tony Wagner would say, the purpose) to create something new and different, and a passion to change the world for the better. The gamers playing *FoldIt* and *eteRNA* were not given any financial reward, but rather points, much like those playing *Angry Birds* or any of the other popular games played on social media sites. They also had a deep sense of pride in knowing they were part of solving one of mankind's biggest challenges. Their efforts could improve life for many individuals around the world who suffer from debilitating, and in some cases life-threatening, diseases that their work may help cure. This, even more than financial reward, drives the innovator.

It's that sense of purpose, and that passion, that also leads people to not only think bigger but to act bigger. I think this passage from Howard Shultz, founder of Starbucks, in his book *Onward*, says it all:

> There is a moment in our lives when we summon the courage to make choices that go against reason, against common sense, and the wise counsel of people we trust. But we lean forward nonetheless because, despite all the risks and rational arguments, we believe that the path we are choosing is the right and best thing to do. We refuse to be bystanders, even if we do not know exactly where our actions will lead. This is the kind of passionate conviction that sparks romances, wins battles, and drives people to pursue dreams others wouldn't dare.

THE INNOVATION CONTINUUM

So, you have the passion, the courage, and the creativity. Now let's spend some time exploring what innovation looks like and more importantly where it can and should play a role in your business. Companies should not innovate just to innovate, but rather to create strategically relevant differentiation in the market. Ask yourself: Where is innovation critical to my day-to-day performance as well as positioning me for the future? What is my strategy and what role does innovation play in achieving my goals, today and tomorrow?

Innovation occurs along a continuum, affecting the entire value chain—from operational efficiency and process improvement to new product development, platform disruptions, and even creating new standards for entire industries.

At the Core

On the far left of the continuum you have innovation in the core of the operation, which helps you do what you already do better. This kind of innovation is often, although not always, iterative as opposed to disruptive. Walmart provides an excellent example of how innovation at the operational level can yield dramatic results. The mega-retailer is able to lower prices and still make money, oftentimes a lot of money, simply by reducing operational costs through supply-chain transformation. Scaled efficiency became the retail giant's strategic differential advantage.

This kind of innovation at the core also works for high-tech companies. When I first arrived at Cisco in 2006, the company's supply chain wasn't positioned to keep pace with global growth. The inability to properly forecast demand made it difficult for contract manufacturers to deliver quality products to the market on time. Cisco hired a new head of manufacturing who deconstructed all of the supply-chain related processes and reworked everything— from demand planning to quality control, even reverse manufacturing (how the company brought products back into inventory for resale into secondary markets). As a result, Cisco was able to better meet growing customer demand, despite uncertainty in a changing marketplace.

Few companies in history have exceeded—or even met—the level of relentless supply-chain discipline demonstrated by Dell in the early 2000s. By making operational excellence (lower cost inventory models, improved manufacturing efficiencies, stream-lined product delivery) a strategic advantage, Dell exceeded market expectations for growth, profitability, and productivity, all while improving customer satisfaction. Dell ultimately set the pace for the industry to follow. Unfortunately, as discussed previously, it failed to continue to innovate and lost its competitive edge.

The strategic questions to ask at this stage on the innovation continuum are:

- "How can we tune our current processes, practices, and systems to make them smarter, better, and faster than they are today?"

- "What can we do to optimize better than our traditional competitors?"

At the Product/Service Level

The next stop on the innovation continuum is new product (or service) development. While operational excellence is always important, it is rarely enough for most companies to remain competitively strong and relevant in the global market over the long term. They need to come up with new products and services that deliver greater market value, build brand loyalty, increase employee pride, satisfy investors, and create partnership opportunities with adjacent businesses.

P&G has historically been the leader in this arena, with bellwether products such as Crest, the world's first fluoride tooth-paste, to teeth-whitening strips. One of P&G's strengths in this area is looking for ideas for new products holistically, which is no small task given the company's size and the number of products it offers around the globe. The teeth-whitening strips are a perfect example.

This new product category was the result of advancements made in its laundry (bleaching), food wrap (film), and paper (glue) lines.

P&G product innovation reframes existing product categories, leading to breakthroughs in market share, profit levels, and consumer acceptance. For example, in 2009, P&G introduced the wrinkle-reducing cream Olay Pro-X. Launching a $40-a-bottle product in the depths of a recession might seem like a questionable strategy, but P&G went ahead because it considered the product a transformational and sustainable innovation—clinically proven to be as effective as its much more expensive prescription counterparts and superior to the company's other anti-aging creams. The cream and related products generated first year sales of $50 million in U.S. food retailers and drugstores alone.

P&G has also been innovative by customizing product formulations to meet the needs of emerging markets. For example, Tide Naturals was introduced in India to solve consumer needs for a lower cost product that could be used by people who wash their clothes by hand. The new product was launched at a price point that is nearly 30 percent less expensive than the legacy Tide product and contains fewer harsh chemicals. By making the Tide brand more accessible and more suitable to Indian consumers, P&G was able to build market share, improve customer loyalty, and more easily gain market acceptance for other products as well.

It doesn't always have to be a new product, just a better product. P&G is the master at what it calls "er" benefits: incremental innovations that make its current products better, easier, and cheaper. Toothpaste that whitens *and* prevents cavities; disposable diapers that fit better *and* keep the baby drier; dishwasher detergent tablets that work for both prewash *and* the wash cycle. Historically, this approach has helped P&G sustain market share with current customers, while enticing additional consumers to try its products. As former P&G CEO A.G. Lafley wrote in the company's 2008 annual report: "We innovate across more categories and on more leading brands than any other consumer products company."

And then there are the game-changing product (or service) introductions. Consider the impact of the iPhone on the mobile device market. The original smartphone completely disrupted the mobile device market—by delivering a product that was not only a phone, but also a camera, a GPS system, a personal planner, a music storage and playback device, you name it. It was also to many a work of art, with a look and feel unlike anything else in the marketplace. But the real game changer was the concept of letting developers offer myriad applications that iPhone owners could pick and choose from to meet their specific needs and interests. As early as the first release, sports fans could access live sports, while foodies could get restaurant recommendations in their neighborhood or wherever they were at the time. Apple also made it easier to tap into the latest social media sites, including Facebook and Twitter. Today, Apple boasts more than 700,000 different apps for the iPhone.

Apple's disruption of the mobile device market paved its way into an existing market where the barriers to entry were high and the established leaders, such as Nokia, were entrenched. Through innovation, Apple soon became the market leader, if not the market's darling, and set the bar that until recently few competitors could rise above. As a result, customers who were perfectly delighted with their current iPhone were happy to stand in line and pay a premium price just to get the next generation product.

The strategic questions to ask at this stage of innovation are:

- "What kinds of new products or product improvements can we deliver that better meet market needs and are superior to what our traditional (and potentially new) competitors offer?"

- "How do we create, capture, and deliver more value to the markets that we already serve?

Companies that do product innovation well can achieve ongoing momentum in the categories in which they currently compete as well as create opportunities to capture value in adjacent markets.

At the Business Model Level

Moving further on the innovation continuum takes us to business model recreation and even disruption. Starbucks is an excellent example. Who would have thought that people would spend five dollars for a cup of gourmet coffee? It's actually not about the coffee—even though Starbucks makes a pretty good one. The Starbucks experience is the innovation that changed—and continues to recreate—the coffeehouse model. Beyond a good cup of coffee, Starbucks provides new ways for consumers to connect, in person or online, with friends, business associates, literally the rest of the digital world. But Starbucks does new products well, too, extending its brand to food, then music, and now high-end kitchen appliances. And in some markets, they are moving beyond the coffeehouse and competing with bars and other establishments that serve adult beverages, extending both the time frame and context of the Starbucks experience.

As I mentioned before, Amazon is the ultimate business model chameleon, first changing how books are bought and sold and now just about everything else, from ladybugs for organic gardeners to haute couture. Becoming e-tailer of just about everything was simply an extension of its existing market model, while Amazon's emergence as a cloud service pioneer came almost by accident. As founder Jeff Bezos explains it, Amazon needed to create a set of application programming interfaces that would stabilize and harden the environment in which its application engineers work, one that would not require them to have as many conversations with the data center team. Originally created to meet an internal need, Amazon quickly realized that if it needed this, others probably did as well, and Amazon Web Services was created. Bezos says Amazon does not do "me too" products well; it looks for opportunities that truly differentiate the company and the value it delivers.

Once again, P&G makes the list of leaders at this stage of the innovation continuum. For example, it recently parlayed its 65 years of experience in home fabric care to disrupt the dry cleaning business model. Two years after a successful test run in Kansas City, P&G opened 11 Tide Dry Cleaner stores in five states in August 2012. P&G did its research (something it does very, very well) and found that consumers were frustrated with limited hours, use of hazardous chemicals, and often dingy locations. In response, P&G created a franchise model that offers earth-friendly technology, drive-through concierge service, 24-hour access, and even text and mobile alerts when clothes are ready for pick-up. Success is yet to be determined, but the concept is certainly appealing to many of us who forget to pick up their clothes until 8 p.m. the night before that all-important business trip.

Business model evolution typically requires answering these strategic questions:

- "Is our business model portfolio robust enough to deliver against today's market performance while creating future market opportunity?"
- "What are the fundamental assumptions behind our business? Are we challenging them often enough?"
- "Can we adapt/change our business model(s) faster than our competitors can create new markets?"

At the Platform Level

Next along the continuum are the platform innovations. Once again, Apple provides the quintessential illustration. Consider the impact of the iPod and iTunes on the entire entertainment industry. Not only did Apple introduce a much more portable and cool-looking device for listening to music, it also launched a new platform for procuring, using, storing, and sharing all sorts of entertainment content. Apple's technology and platform innovation led many consumers to stop buying CDs and replace them with digitized MP3 files.

The result of disruptive innovation at the platform level is that the market is really never the same—because it changes where and how value is created, and in turn, changes the fundamentals of the business. When platform innovations hit, they have a profound impact on the industries and the markets they touch. Consider how LinkedIn has changed the way businesspeople network. Created to change how professionals manage their business contacts, the social media site has dramatically altered how recruiters find prospects and how job seekers look for work. In turn, LinkedIn had significant implications for businesses and industries that previously served those markets. LinkedIn now has more than 175 million registered users in more than 200 countries and territories around the globe.

Platform innovations are generated by asking strategic questions:

- "How do we leverage our product and technology platforms to disrupt entire markets?"
- "How do we disintermediate competitors in the process?"

At the Standards and Protocols Level

The final stop on this continuum is where some companies change entire industries with the introduction of protocols and standards, often in collaboration with competitors. Consider how the introduction of scanning technology changed the grocery industry. The movement was ushered in by the leaders of the largest grocery store chains that each wanted to move people through their checkout lines faster. While they were competitors, they realized that to achieve their common objective they should work together to increase the adoption and use of industry standards—in this case the UPC code, which could then enable products to be scanned by checkout clerks. The ubiquitous nature of the UPC code on grocery products today has yielded benefits far beyond checkouts, from seamless product replenishment to better recall management.

At the turn of the century, leaders of five of the world's largest healthcare manufacturers embarked on a similar collaborative effort. A study had identified billions of dollars in waste caused by highly manual and inaccurate supply-chain processes. To address this problem, Johnson & Johnson, Medtronic, GE, Baxter, and Abbott joined together to create an Internet trading exchange that would standardize how hospitals purchase products from not only the five founding companies, but ideally from all of their suppliers. Today, Global Healthcare Exchange (GHX) is owned by 20 companies, many of whom are competitors, representing both the buy and sell side of the healthcare supply chain. GHX is used by most U.S. hospitals, as well as healthcare providers in Canada and Europe, to purchase the majority of their medical-surgical supplies. Documented savings are well into billions of dollars.

The strategic question to ask at this stage of innovation:

- "How do we collaborate with our ecosystem partners to set new standards (and protocols) for an entire industry?"

CREATING A CULTURE OF INNOVATION IN ORGANIZATIONS

Building a culture of innovation begins with a visionary leader who knows what direction to go and is willing to make hard decisions to change the course of her company. It also requires an environment where people are encouraged to look at the world through more empathetic eyes, to ask different questions, and to be open to new solutions. It's about "what could be," not about "what is." And as discussed earlier, it requires a team powered by a sense of purpose to create something uniquely valuable for the company and more importantly the world.

The challenge for most leaders is that innovation is one of the more opaque activities that companies undertake—no one really knows when these kinds of efforts or initiatives will take off.

According to Chris Malloy, associate professor and Marvin Bower Fellow at Harvard Business School, innovation is the hardest thing on a balance sheet or an income statement to measure, and yet it can have a huge impact on a company's overall value. Malloy notes that some companies, like Apple, are considerably better than others at converting investments in innovation into product and revenue growth (2012). Amazon is as well, reinventing its business model every three to four years: from online bookseller and e-tailer to device dealer and now cloud-service broker. How do companies like Amazon and Apple achieve such transformational success? Their leaders fully appreciate that change is a constant imperative, and so they have infused their organizations with both the flexibility to seize new opportunities quickly and the resilience to weather the accompanying ups and downs.

But it takes more than flexibility and resilience to remain competitive in a volatile global market. Corporations need to make experimentation and exploration the norm, not the exception. A good example is Google, where engineers are encouraged to spend 20 percent of their time working on company projects that they find personally meaningful. When work has meaning, it sparks creativity as well as the passion to go that extra mile. Many of Google's most innovative technologies, including Gmail and Google News, have their origins in what is known as 20 percent time.

How does this tinkering approach to innovation turn into successful businesses at Google? When seeking to make broad changes across the organization, an engineer will form a group of like-minded individuals who are equally committed to the idea and willing to help convince the rest of the organization to support it. Often these groups (called grouplets) operate with no budget and no real decision-making authority. But Google is structured specifically to allow the best ideas to spread fast. If a grouplet grows large enough and gains enough internal support, the idea becomes reality. The concept is simple but highly powerful: If you give good engineers the chance to apply their passion and their capabilities to their work and to the company, they will do what it takes to make amazing innovations happen. As a result, the company has mastered how to capture early mover advantage: with ideas, with initiatives, with product launches, with new platform plays, and with business model evolutions. Self-organization works.

Granted, not every company is a Google, an Amazon, or an Apple. But leaders of other mere mortal corporations can still learn from their approach to innovation. At the individual level, as Tony Wagner notes, it is about play, purpose, and passion. But at the organization level, it's about process, too. Innovation is not just about smart and passionate people brainstorming—although that's certainly an important and necessary element. Innovation takes foresight, discipline, and courage to expect different results by doing things differently, often dramatically different, as opposed to the old definition of insanity: doing the same thing and expecting different results. You need to put frameworks and processes in place to bring order to the chaos, to bring structure to the unstructured, and to bring value to smart ideas. Think back to the discussion in chapter 2 about how Amazon CEO Jeff Bezos makes the case for applying some rules to the process of brainstorming. It's the same concept.

Make Innovation Strategic

What companies like Apple and other formidable innovators such as Google, P&G, Amazon, Cisco, and Ericsson have in common is that they continually differentiate themselves from the competition in the markets they serve by making innovation integral to their strategy. By gathering market intelligence and deconstructing their competitors' business models, companies can construct disruptive innovations that generate value for the market and for the company. They take the time to carefully delineate how their companies will respond to market shifts, new technologies, disruptive startups, or competitor improvements in core business offerings. So rather than pull last year's strategy off the shelf, freshen it up a bit, and hit "save as," they hold a series of defining conversations to flesh out what is, what isn't, and most importantly, what should be.

These organizations stand out from others in that they encourage idea generation and the reinvention process. They have established systems for vetting their innovation funnels and determining which ideas are worthy of incubation and investment. They rigorously monitor the competitive landscape and foster the best-of-the-best in terms of concept generation. Competitors, peers, and customers respect these companies for making an impact on an industry and a difference for society. In the same way that the iPhone changed the mobile phone business forever, their innovations are seen as the founding technologies in their respective areas. And most importantly, the senior leaders of these organizations are deliberate in how they build organizations (and cultures) that sustain innovative value over time.

INNOVATION IN PARALLEL: IN THE CORE AND AT THE EDGE

As we have discussed, one of the core competencies of leaders, especially at the global level, is the ability to focus on multiple—and often seemingly conflicting—priorities. When it comes to innovation, this is particularly important. Successful leaders and their companies must sustain value through innovations at the core to keep the business successful today, while at the same time creating new value for the future by innovating at the edge.

Consider Starbucks again. While the company continues to make inroads into new markets (both in terms of products and geographies), it must still be very good at buying coffee, fresh dairy, paper products, and other merchandise, and distributing them to stores around the world, to ensure that the Starbucks experience in Tokyo or Moscow or New Delhi is as equally delightful as it is at the company's original stores in Seattle. But Starbucks simultaneously spends time innovating at the edge, which, for example, led to the creation of the Starbucks Entertainment division and the Hear Music brand that is now marketing books, music, and film.

Like Starbucks, it is critical to understand where, when, and how your company must innovate to stay relevant and create new levels of value, because while all forms of innovation along the continuum are important, not all innovations will deliver the same returns. Innovation at the core increases the organization's ability to sustain business by tuning the current business model and operating engine(s). Innovation at the edge increases the organization's ability to create entirely new revenue streams.

Innovations at the core are often developed in response to competitive threats to the core business model. Most are iterative: continual but relatively small improvements that typically achieve productivity gains by optimizing operational processes. They are the ongoing improvements necessary to build on past successes and are often designed to preserve margins by reducing costs.

So, with considerable financial pressures at play, how do you create room for disruptive innovation at the edge? And a more important question: How can companies do both? Unfortunately, many don't. But why?

It is partly because companies must compete in the short-term, and in doing so they often lose patience in dealing with the dynamics of longer-term investments in innovation. Searching for breakthrough innovation is expensive and time consuming; product and service-line extensions can help the bottom line immediately, without long incubation cycles that can drain resources (and potentially margins) in the short run.

Second, past success gets in the way. Innovation is particularly challenging for those companies that have long-standing, traditionally successful business models that produce predictable streams of revenue quarter over quarter, year over year. Investment in innovation—particularly when it competes with investments that could otherwise be leveraged to run the primary business (enhance the base infrastructure, improve process and technology, hire the best engineers, expand the global footprint)—is hard for many companies to justify, especially when the effort may or may not generate revenue for several quarters, if not years, into the future.

Game-changing innovators are often confronted with traditional business case or return-on-investment questions. Why would I give you a dollar toward your unproven idea when I can reinvest that dollar in something I know works? The problem is, as I have said, what worked before may no longer work, and may actually thwart success in the future. We've all heard it before, especially from larger scale, traditionally successful companies that argue, "Hope is not a strategy." I get that, but that does not mean you can't build the business case for innovation. It just means innovation is not a traditional business case.

I liken it to an investment portfolio. Does it make sense just to invest in blue-chip stocks that provide a nearly guaranteed— although relatively small—return, or should you diversify your portfolio and set aside some funds for riskier but potentially higher yield investments? As any good investment advisor would tell you, you need to have a strategy and be prepared to execute on that strategy versus acting out of fear or loyalty. Using the investment analogy, if you have a growth strategy, then why would you invest only in value stocks? What does your strategy say about when you should continue to hold on to a stock, especially when it is not yet proving profitable, when you should sell, and when you should buy more?

It's the same for companies that also need to know when they should continue to invest in a particular innovation initiative, when they should move on, and when they should up their investment to the necessary level to create a viable business offering. The biggest question is in knowing how much bloodletting has to go on before the bleeding edge gives birth to something of long-term value or when it needs to be put out of its misery. A classic example of a company that gave up too soon on innovation is Kodak. It created the technology behind the digital camera, but failed to pursue an aggressive market strategy for fear of cannibalizing its cash cow— the film business. Not surprisingly, the digital business did not deliver results fast enough and Kodak lost interest.

Third, as we discussed in the previous chapter on essential traits, most notably the experimental mind section, the creative process depends upon learning from your mistakes. Unfortunately, many organizations are still more comfortable doing what they have always done because they know what to expect. But it's not about "if this happens, then we can expect that." It's about "let's see what happens when we do this." The decision to try this, and not that, is based on observation and insights, not just positive thinking. And success ultimately depends on the ability to move quickly when you discover something new that works. In other words, you need to know when and how to bring innovation at the edge into the fold.

For many innovative products or services, you need to incubate them and nurture them until they are ready for prime time. Even an innovation that has proven itself worthy of market launch often needs to be held back until you can be sure all of the necessary elements are in place, including market readiness, to ensure its success. For example, the biggest game changers—the products that have the most market potential—often experience slow initial market traction; only the brave early adopters are ready to give them a try. As a result, the company's core salesforce may not put adequate effort behind the new products, instead focusing on proven sales leaders that will help them make their quotas. Then, in the face of disappointing sales, the company may be tempted to give up on the new product. In these cases, it is sometimes better to have a dedicated salesforce just for your new product innovation until it can stand on its own as part of the company's full portfolio.

And fourth, out-of-the-box innovation is challenging for most companies. By definition, it requires individuals (and organizations) to see the world differently, to ask new questions, and to think in new ways. Just as innovation occurs on a continuum, so does the way people think about innovation. Those responsible for the operations of the core business think about innovation more incrementally, while those working on the edge think in terms of transformation. Core innovators, by default, need to stay focused on what will generate the kinds of returns that employers, shareholders, and financial markets require today. But to remain relevant in a fast-changing and hyper-competitive world, companies need to nurture people who have aspirations (and capabilities) to think beyond, sometimes way beyond, the current state.

At Cisco, we spent a considerable amount of time thinking about what the future would look like and where we wanted Cisco to play. As chief talent officer, my job was to determine what kind of leadership skills would be required in the future to achieve our strategic objectives and then to plan in reverse how we should begin developing those leaders today. When we identified individuals for promotion, we deliberately considered what they were doing today to help create that future state, in addition to what they were doing to ensure solid performance today.

For this reason, leaders have to build organizations that are capable of acting like a startup, while still operating efficiently on a global scale. They require very different business models and organizational structures, staffed with people who have equally different skill sets, and yet who are capable of innovating wherever they are on the continuum—at the core, on the edge, or somewhere in between.

Although innovations at the core and on the edge are happening in vastly different worlds, they are increasingly dependent upon one another. That's what's so ironic about the dynamic of innovating in parallel. Until relatively recently, larger, more structured corporate environments were often hostile to innovation, but now they provide exactly the kinds of resources— from operational scale and capital to the brand stature necessary to attract business partners—that entrepreneurial individuals depend upon both initially and for the long-term survival of their creative ideas. The core business, meanwhile, depends upon continual innovation on the edge to remain relevant and competitive in a fast-changing and hyper-competitive market.

The challenge for leaders is how to get those living at the core to understand the importance of the investment on the edge, and how to help incorporate innovation into the core business when it's time. This can be particularly challenging when innovation is less about new products or technology and more about business model and market disruption. Leaders need to create environments where those living fully at the core welcome (or at least openly accept) the significant disruption to their world that innovation can create. You are not just talking about creating a new product to sell or a new market to seize—you are talking about rocking their worlds and their comfort zones.

For the innovator on the edge, hope is, if not a strategy, then at least a mindset. It's about changing the world and designing futuristic business and organizational models that probably have little to do with running the business today. But for those living at the core, that's what it's all about: keeping the business going while continually looking for new ways to extract more profits from the current operations, products, and solutions. As a result, different standards and measures must be used to manage their respective progress and success.

The problem is that many leaders fall back on the old key performance indicators that work for the core business to evaluate innovation because there is no guidebook to tell them what else to use. Think about it: How can you have a pre-established set of standards to assess what has essentially not yet been created? What you can do is take the time to decide what's important to you as you embark on the innovative adventure, and decide how you will evaluate whether you are keeping true to those values as you move forward.

The critical players to achieving a peaceful and comple-mentary coexistence between those who are focused on today's realities and those who prioritize tomorrow's possibilities are the value translators: people who understand and appreciate the necessity and messiness of work on the edge and yet can explain the value and relevancy in terms that make sense to those who live in the much more structured and regimented world of sales quotas and quarterly earnings. In turn, they help innovators appreciate how profitability and revenue growth at the core are essential to funding new growth ventures.

Countless companies contend that innovation is among their core values, but few actually take the time to design the organization's structure and deliberately create the culture required to foster innovation. This is not about tinkering but rather about taking a systematic approach to creating the right framework, processes, and rewards. Is your company effectively structured for innovation? The answer will depend on your business strategy and where your organization is in its life cycle. It's easier for startups to innovate. They either innovate or die. But as companies get larger, and more mature, they must put more controls in place to replicate and scale processes, which can put stress on the more innovative aspects of their organizations. Larger companies solve this dilemma by creating innovation labs or separate R&D functions; smaller companies often rely on joint ventures to keep innovation alive on the side. Here are some things to consider that will help make innovation a core competency for your organization.

Ask yourself:

- What does innovation mean to your organization?
- How ambitious are your objectives for innovation?
- How are you managing your innovation portfolio?
- How is your organization allocating its investments? In safe bets in the core? In less sure opportunities in adjacent spaces? In higher risk initiatives at the edge?

Define Your Destination

Target a healthy balance of innovation at the core business, in adjacent products or markets, and at the transformational edge.

Make Culture Matter

While many companies still see culture as secondary to success, the wrong culture can kill the best strategy. As a leader, it is your responsibility to forge a culture that accepts and rewards open-ended, messy problem solving, a topic we will explore further in the next chapter. It begins by fostering innovator-focused values: visioning; experimentation; freedom to fail; tolerance for differences of opinion; and collaboration.

Leverage Collaboration

Collaboration is another of those oft-touted, rarely practiced concepts. In many companies, collaboration actually takes the form of classic passive-aggressive behavior. People sit in a room, say they agree to collaborate, nod their heads as different ideas are expressed and decisions are made, only to leave still holding fast to their individual points of view and acting accordingly. It's not surprising when you consider what Tony Wagner's work pointed out earlier. We are raised, at least in Western societies, to prioritize individual performance. The forced ranking performance review systems used by so many companies only exacerbate the problem. If you grade on a curve, 30 percent of your employees will have a strong sense of accomplishment and recognition, leaving 70 percent (even those who are told they are doing a good job) feeling disappointed, unappreciated, and, at worst, unmotivated.

Open collaboration is a critical component to creating a culture of innovation. If you are going to achieve different outcomes, you must do things differently, sometimes very differently. And that can require different people with very different perspectives collaborating, often on a global scale.

By definition, innovation is an iterative and collaborative process. One person may have a kernel of an idea that others build on, while an integrative thinker will connect the dots and offer up another perspective, and the process repeats itself. In the end, you likely have a much better solution, one that can only be attributed to the team and the process, not to an individual. This is in contrast to the more traditional rules of an industrial age where a chosen few (typically the most senior leaders) went behind closed doors to solve the company's biggest strategic challenges. Given today's market expectations, global competitive pressures, and pace of change, that approach is not just outdated and unacceptable (to employees, customers, and business partners), it's also unwise. Rarely can a limited few come up with the best solutions. Collaboration must happen up and down the organization and across all disciplines. That's when exciting things happen.

Ask yourself:

- Are you structured for growth and innovation? Are your best innovators (whether process, product, business model, or platform) aligned around your biggest opportunity (or need)?

- How do you put the best minds in the room to ask tough questions and solve the most pressing business opportunities?

- How do you encourage these individuals, at times, to put their own ideas aside in the interest of bringing forth the best ideas?

- How do you let go of hierarchical power to encourage the best ideas to flourish from any place and at any level?

Align the Stars

You must have the right people in the right work, in the right environment, and with the right incentives. Multitasking is great for some jobs, but those organizations that set the stage for successful innovation appreciate the fact that transformational innovation requires undivided attention. Give your innovators the opportunity to wake up every day and focus on creating and delivering new forms of value.

Remember, too, that innovators are motivated differently from those working on the core business. While the typical salesperson is driven by short-term financial incentives, on-the-edge innovators are working on projects that do not fit neatly into quarterly or even annual cycles. If you want to provide a financial reward, how about offering to share a small percentage of the profits if a project takes off? Perhaps even more appropriate is the opportunity to keep working on innovation. As Daniel Pink writes in his book *Drive*, creative people are motivated by autonomy, opportunities to develop mastery, and a sense of purpose. Scott Anthony says, "This applies in spades to [corporate] catalysts" (Anthony, 2012).

Performance and reward systems must deliberately recognize those behaviors that drive new ways of doing things, that position innovators and corporate catalysts as symbolic heroes of the company. Don't get me wrong. It's not that innovators are better than traditional performers, or vice versa—you need both. You also need a system of rewards and recognition that encourages both behaviors.

Ask yourself:

- How does your performance system drive growth, productivity, and innovation?
- Do you customize your compensation strategies to align with desired behaviors and outcomes?
- How are ideas (good or bad) encouraged, reinforced, learned from, and rewarded?

Develop Your Innovation Talk Track

Ideally, the leader can serve as the value translator, providing the bigger picture view of the company's strategic long- and short-term goals and how various activities at the core and on the edge complement one another. If not, it is up to the leader to ensure that there are value translators on the leadership team and situated strategically in the organization. As innovations are brought into the core, leaders and their value translators need to remind the organization of the history and evolution of the idea so that they can see the value and be more receptive to new innovation initiatives. And when there are failures, make sure to remind the company of what was learned in the process and how those lessons will serve the company going forward.

> **Ask yourself:**
> - What is the leadership of the organization saying about innovation?
> - How is the organization talking about innovation?
> - What are the stories that are repeated as examples?
> - What are the key strategic and operational messages that drive organizational focus?

LEADERSHIP ON THE EDGE

Just as innovations fall on a continuum, so do leaders. My experience is that only a small percentage of leaders truly live on the edge themselves. These game-changing leaders display the unique ability to anticipate market transitions. They look out on a time horizon that is much longer than the average leader. They are often restless and in search of change. They make strategic moves that are often several steps ahead of everyone else. If you reflect back on our chess game analogy, these are the leaders who are moving pieces in a game that has not even started. These are the leaders who are described as "before their time." They envision the future and then figure out what they need to do today to get to where they want to be tomorrow. They go even further and ask: "What would it look like if we were to change what the future looks like?" And in most cases they rely on value translators to help people make sense of their vision.

Other leaders excel as value creators, which is a step beyond value translators. As leaders, these individuals take the (what often seems like crazy) ideas of the game changers and figure out how to generate real value, for the market and for their companies. They position organizations for strategic agility and the change required to adjust to a faster-moving world. As such, they fully appreciate the need for innovation at the edge and know when and how it can and should be brought into the core. They can weave an idea into viable business plans that can satisfy even the most fact-focused CFO and create the organizational structure to bring those ideas into fruition, in a timely and cost-effective manner.

Cisco's Marthin DeBeer is the quintessential value creator. A true innovator at heart, he recognizes the realities of innovation. First of all, he says, you have to understand the full life cycle of innovation and how it ties to the organization's priorities, today and tomorrow. As he puts it, "you have to know where the puck is going" and continually ensure that others in the company understand the opportunities, the timelines, and the connections to the business priorities. Times change, focus changes, and the first time the business is under pressure to reduce OPEX, if you have not made the appropriate connections, innovative programs are often the first to get cut. He adds emphatically that those in charge of innovation also need to be more like venture capitalists and not become too attached to their own ideas. If the timing is not right, if the market is not ideal, you have to be willing to cut the cord.

The value creators are often the true experimenters in the company: taking ideas and vetting them, and then vetting them again, for viability. Game-changing executives also rely on the value creators to put healthy systems in place for managing risk, so that the organization tolerates and even supports risk when it makes sense, but can also eliminate risk when necessary.

All the while, companies need to have members of their leadership teams whose job and skill sets are focused on the day-to-day operating performance of the business; those who can make sure the company stays profitable today in order to invest in the future. These large-scale operators, as I call them, work on a much shorter time horizon and focus their impact on optimizing their organizations for efficiency. They are often exceptional at running large operations where typically a heavy analytical approach to business management is required. These are the leaders who continually diagnose issues and focus on practical innovations that strengthen profitability and productivity in the core business model. These leaders are excellent at building and running the engine, at achieving short-term benchmarks, and at rigorously collecting and analyzing performance data to identify opportunities for business and operating improvement. While these leaders may not transform markets or industries, they will transform the core processes that underlie the infrastructure of the business. And in doing so, they will position the organization to achieve stretch targets on productivity, return on capital, and quarterly deliverables.

Today's organizations must constantly seek competitive advantage without disrupting daily operations. The art of leadership comes in creating the right balance of capabilities—between game changers, value creators, and large-scale operators. I can't underscore enough the importance of managing leadership talent deliberately and closely. Just as you manage your product and innovation portfolios, so too should you manage your leadership talent portfolio. The balanced allocation of leadership capabilities will not only yield higher business performance today, but it will also bring a nimbleness to adapt to, adjust, and implement initiatives for the future.

All of this requires nothing short of systemic change for many businesses to support and sustain invention, reinvention, and transformation. Innovation doesn't just happen, nor is it simply nice to have. Stop. Think.

Ask yourself:

- Where is innovation occurring in your organization?
- Where should it occur?
- What can you do as a leader to tear down barriers that stifle creativity?
- How can you create the kind of culture necessary to ensure you even have a future?
- Do you have the appropriate distribution of game changers, value creators, and large-scale operators to effectively execute your strategy?

In the next chapter, we will explore why most existing talent management systems and business schools get a failing grade when it comes to developing the kind of leaders needed to foster innovation that meets the demands of a highly dynamic and diverse global business environment. You'll also learn why it is no one's fault or responsibility, other than yours.

CHAPTER 6

Develop Leadership: Executives, Take Charge!

By now, I hope I have convinced you that the world is changing, and so is what it takes to be a truly global leader. The challenge before you is a gap in leadership capabilities—on both the individual and organizational level—to meet the demands of a complex global economy. As Harold Stock, CEO, Grünenthal Group, stated in the Conference Board's CEO Challenge 2012 Report "What keeps me up at night is how to get the best talent and create the environment for the best talent to thrive. I think if you've got that, you can take on every challenge." Addressing this need will require the same amount of commitment and attention that CEOs need to put toward redesigning their organizational and business models. In fact, it requires a fundamentally different approach than we have traditionally taken to developing leadership and talent systems. After all, if the world is changing, if the nature of leadership is changing, and if business models are changing, then why shouldn't our approach to how we develop leadership in our organizations change as well? We've already talked about how many of the business models still in place in corporations and businesses today were designed to address the productivity problems of an industrial economy, not the dynamic realities of an information economy. But while many business leaders are waking up to this reality, they continue to turn to leadership development systems that were designed to support the old models and are well past their "sell by" dates.

I also believe that no one owns this problem more than global CEOs. First, the success of their organizations, and in many cases, their own careers and professional legacies, depends upon it. As discussed in detail in the prior chapter, business leaders need to make sure that their companies can remain competitive in a world where there are new competitors emerging every day, from geographic regions not previously on their radar—at least not as competitive threats—with products and solutions they never envisioned. Therein lies the problem. How do you prepare leaders for something that is anything but well defined?

Larry Bossidy, former CEO of AlliedSignal, wrote convincingly about the topic of CEO responsibility as early as 2001 in a *Harvard Business Review* article entitled: "The Job No CEO Should Delegate." As he explained, "Many executives have neglected a personal involvement, accountability, and initiative in developing leaders within their organizations. But because it is full of unknowns, of unpredictability, it deserves more time than anything else you do as a CEO." If you question the return on investing this much time and energy in what most CEOs delegate to their HR departments, consider the results Bossidy achieved. In less than a decade, AlliedSignal provided nearly a ninefold return for stockholders, tripled its operating margins, and achieved a 28 percent return on equity. Bossidy adds that "the greatest sign of our success was the extraordinary quality of our management team" and says he is "convinced that AlliedSignal's success was due in large part to the amount of time and emotional commitment [he] devoted to leadership development" (2001).

LEADERSHIP DEVELOPMENT IN CRISIS

If you are still not convinced, stay with me. The field of leadership development is in crisis, and what I am going to say next will no doubt upset some of those who have dedicated their work to teaching, training, or consulting. I mean no disrespect. What I hope to do is provide a wake-up call to those executives whose companies collectively spend billions of dollars each year on leadership development and to those in charge of providing education and development services but who are not achieving the enduring level of success required or desired. Executives need to take charge, and build talent development systems that will ensure their investments in other critical areas of their business pay off.

What concerns me most is that many of those offering leadership development programs are not aware that their approaches no longer fit the needs of a diverse and highly fluid marketplace. They are failing to meet the needs of their customers. But what's the problem? There is certainly no shortage of leadership development programs promising to teach you how to anticipate what comes next, to lead globally and cross-culturally, and to deal with ambiguity and complexity. They claim they are innovative, context relevant, and collaborative. Unfortunately, that has rarely been my experience.

While at Cisco, I had responsibility for the company's executive development strategies. Early in my tenure as the chief talent officer, I asked my executive-education organization to identify some potential providers to help us develop our current and emerging leaders. We were looking for partners who would truly collaborate with us, both in the design and the delivery of programs and initiatives that would position Cisco for the future. As discussed previously, Cisco was undertaking an aggressive globalisation effort to bring the company and its people closer to new markets, to attract new talent, and to better understand customer needs. To accomplish this, we needed innovative approaches to creating learning opportunities for leaders in the field and in the context of their current work: leadership viability labs, if you will, not classroom-based training programs that separate the learning environment from the real world. To do this, we needed a strategic partner, not a vendor.

The team scoured the globe, talking with nearly 100 different providers, including universities and business schools, executive-education programs, even leadership-focused think tanks, and came up close to empty. There were just a few that even understood what we were trying to do. Only two university programs even came close.

Harvard Business School was actually working on a program that would likely have fit our needs, but at the time, it was still more aspiration than reality. MBA students enrolled in the **Field Immersion Experiences for Leadership Development (FIELD)** curriculum, which was launched in January 2011, work in teams to design a new product or service for a global partner, primarily in emerging markets. In the process of doing this, students learn about how business processes, capabilities, institutions, and customers, among other things, vary across different markets.

During my travels in India, I met with the dean at the **India School of Business** in Hyderabad. Founded by two consultants from McKinsey & Co., the school provides what its website calls "market-centric education," with many of the faculty having significant experience in both the corporate and academic worlds. One of the more unique aspects is that its postgraduate education programs are taught with a strong vertical focus in specific disciplines, such as HR and finance, and an emphasis on issues critical to emerging markets, including affordable housing, entrepreneurship, and innovation. More than anything, I was impressed with the dean's first question to me: "What is your company trying to solve and how can we partner?" He did not lead by proposing pre-existing programs. Our needs—and the needs of a changing global marketplace—were paramount.

Deloitte's Center for the Edge was one of the few consultancy practices that could speak our language. Its work is based on actual field studies—the real world if you will. Deloitte apparently has been listening to its customers. Bill Pelster, a principal and talent-development leader at Deloitte, put it this way: "The overriding theme of what I've been hearing from clients recently is that they're a bit stunned—shocked, actually—at how the leadership-development programs they'd had in place were not able to meet the needs of their business as we've gone through these tremendously disruptive economic changes over the past few years" (McIlvaine, 2010).

Given the limited choices, we decided our best option was to build an internal consulting team to create exactly what we needed, which was something very different from what was generally available in the marketplace. This new team designed business-relevant leadership models and hands-on programs. These programs would develop leadership capabilities that both individual performers and the organization as a whole would need to achieve our specific strategic objectives. For example, as a high-tech company that needed to be faster to market than our competitors, we looked at how to develop leadership competencies around shaping market strategy, disruptive innovation, and collaboration. We'll explore some of the concepts and programs later in this chapter.

So, why couldn't we find what we were looking for, either in existing programs or through a collaborative partner? And why was our challenge indicative of what so many other companies experience? Let me tell you about something that happened just this week: I received a proposal from the dean of a top business school. I had previously met with the dean and his team to discuss a company's needs around leadership development. Once again, I was looking for a provider that could help us develop innovative action learning methodologies within the global context in which the leaders operated—in essence, the viability lab concept I mentioned before. The dean was honestly excited about the request and left assuring me that his team would come back with a customized approach. What was in the proposal? A four-hour professor-led didactic session on various topics right out of the business school catalog. Clearly, we have a different definition of customization. To me, it is all about providing what I need to make my business better. To the dean and many of his colleagues, it appears to be more about bringing what they already have and then customizing those programs and materials to meet varied timing or pricing requirements. I wasn't surprised. But I was disappointed.

Business Schools Are Not the Answer

Businesspeople continue to call on leading business schools for leadership development support; after all, who ever got fired for hiring names like Duke, INSEAD, or the London School of Business? But many people have been disappointed because the approach—and more importantly the results—of executive education don't match what organizations need. In essence, leadership development in the academic world doesn't develop leaders in the business world. There are many reasons why this may be happening: mismatched incentives, limited perspectives, lack of access and relevancy, and outdated business and instructional models.

The academic system traditionally encourages proliferation of a particular university's or academic's point of view, which can discourage collaboration or customization. Universities make money by building once and selling to many, and professors are rewarded for publishing, not teaching. As long as these remain the incentives, the behaviors will not change. I challenge not just the higher educational system, but also the students and businesses that rely upon them to seek a new business model that can drive mutual benefits.

This new model may not be generally well-received, but it's coming. Commenting during a roundtable discussion hosted by TIME International at the February 2013 World Economic forum in Davos, Harvard Business Professor Clayton Christensen said, "What is really hard for us to do is look down at the bottom of the market and see a business model coming at us—which is, we don't need MBAs anymore...Somehow what is not known about a different business model scares us to death" (Wolverson, 2013).

Welcome or not, it's bound to happen; it's just a matter of when. The complexity of the problems facing businesses—if not the world—today will require networks of people who can look at the issues from various viewpoints and disciplines. An MBA graduate will bring a valuable point of view to the discussion, but it is just one point of view. Complexity demands creativity, so invite the artists for an understanding of how humans relate; bring in the anthropologists, the sociologists, and of course the psychologists; for the government policy implications, add political scientists to the mix; and the list goes on. At the very least, why not add art, anthropology, political science, and other nonbusiness courses to the leadership curriculum? Companies need broader thinking beyond the traditional business school course of study. They need something closer to the liberal arts model, but with a more purposeful and global business focus.

It's one of the reasons why I believe programs with models similar to Stanford's d.school are the future of executive education. The program brings together people from diverse backgrounds who build upon each other's thinking, taking them to a place that founder David Kelly says "you just can't get to with one mind" (CBS Interactive, 2013). The problem is, as long as the primary objective of academic institutions is to generate, protect, and sell their own knowledge capital, their own way of thinking, they will not be motivated to co-create. As time goes on, and the world demands new, more collaborative ways of thinking and problem solving, the traditional academic model will become less and less valuable to the executive leadership marketplace.

Research Relevancy

More often than not, business school and executive education classes are taught by professors who are shackled to a tenure system where *publish or perish* is the norm. Tenure is the metric of success and it is not granted for the ability to develop leadership capabilities in others or for creating high performing organizations, but rather for the ability to make a contribution to scholarly, peer-reviewed journals. Don't get me wrong. I respect the peer-review system. It raises the quality of the content and keeps authors honest, something that can be missing in the commercial business press, and worse yet in social media, where anyone can publish just about anything without requisite oversight or fact checking. So, the concept of peer-reviewed literature is sound and should be respected; the problem comes down to how effectively the research can be applied to today's global business environment, which is a function of speed, access, and applicability.

Let's first consider the research being reviewed. Academic research produces what is essentially pure—as opposed to real world, field-tested knowledge. Pure research is good stuff. But it is less relevant to a global leader whose world is anything but pure. In the process of scientific or academic research, it is important to control the variables. But it's the variables—multiple variables, compounding variables, completely unexpected and unimagined variables—that the global business leader has to deal with on a continual basis. How do you control variables that you have never considered? How can research be disseminated in a manner that business leaders can apply to a rapidly changing, interdependent, and highly unpredictable world? Academia needs to be more relevant to business, but business also needs to understand how to put the research to use in context.

Second, the researchers themselves and those who are reviewing the literature are usually career academicians, who, while predominantly of high intellectual caliber, come from the same discipline and perspective and have not had recent, if any, practical business experience. Most have only experienced the industry vicariously through the eyes of their students. How many professors have held a senior leadership position in a corporate setting? How many of them have had to make tough business decisions—the ones that could get them fired—or make tough tradeoffs? Even if they worked in industry before, how many could succeed in today's far more global, far more ambiguous business environment? There are exceptions, both in terms of individuals and institutions, but it is still not the norm.

Then, there is the question of when and how that knowledge can be accessed by business leaders. Peer-reviewed journals, by virtue of the meticulous examination process they must follow, take much longer to be published than articles in the business press. The quality is probably better, but the value is diminished over time, which will become an increasingly critical factor. I am pleased that more peer-reviewed journals are being distributed online, but the content is usually not available until the physical book is out, and it is still costly. The highly specialized nature of the content also makes it hard to connect the findings, the dots if you will, across various disciplines to drive the innovation process.

Finally, when choosing research topics, they are often generated out of the curiosity of the academic researcher, as opposed to what business leaders recommend or need, unless of course they are willing to fund the research. I am not saying that the chosen topics are bad, but they still tend to be driven more by the likelihood to be published, rather than to change a business or industry. Again, these are generalities and should be seen as a discussion about the connection between academic research and the lack of applicability in business leadership development.

Consider all of this together and how it plays differently in the business world, where value is driven by factors such as how fast a product or service can get to market and how well it is received by customers. Does it meet their needs? Is it relevant to their world? Did they receive it not just *on* time, but *in* time to make a difference? If product managers cannot answer these questions in the affirmative, they will likely lose their jobs. In academia, job security is less about whether you delivered value to the end customer.

DISRUPT THE MODEL

The academic world remains relatively closed, compared to a growing trend toward more open and collaborative networks in the business world. Sure, there are alliances between different colleges and universities and the disciplines within those institutions, and even some notable business-academic partnerships. The Harvard FIELD program is a prime example of the latter, linking students with business partners. But overall, the academic world is still a closed society, with a high admission price—be it tuition, sponsorship, or endowment—and even those come with restrictions. Since the academic system as a whole provides a "one for many" approach, how could you expect your leaders to come back to the organization with knowledge in context? We have an opportunity to work together to make this better.

I'm not dismissing the financial realities of running a high quality academic institution. But think what we could accomplish if we could overlay the rigor and exploratory nature of academic research on top of the new business models that support shared learning and innovation across connected practitioner ecosystems. How can we disrupt the academic business platform and create quality education—maybe even something that approaches the open source model—that still creates value for all involved? How can we reward academic researchers for both the quality of their work and their ability (and willingness) to co-create and share knowledge? There are growing movements toward open access and open knowledge: graduate students and so-called recovering academics refusing to publish or review any research that is in a closed journal. Even some of the most notable institutions, beginning with Harvard in 2008, have adopted open-access policies, but researchers can still request that their work not be subject to free distribution if the journals forbid it.

I believe these movements will only grow stronger, as a generation that has grown up sharing everything, and expecting everything to be shared, assumes more influential roles in business and society. But simply demanding open access is not enough. We need a new business model around knowledge itself. A business model based on selling knowledge no longer works in an age when information is increasingly free and accessible. Knowledge should no longer be treated as a stand-alone product; the value to the marketplace is the ability to share that knowledge in a manner that allows others to apply it, enhance it, and create even greater value from it. How does this translate to those in the business of developing leadership? What can we learn from companies like Red Hat that make their software and their code available, at no cost, even to competitors, and yet still manage to attract paying customers and make a profit? What can we learn from companies like Kodak that held on too tightly to its highly profitable chemical-based film and paper manufacturing business and missed the opportunity to capitalize on the move to digital photography—even though it invented the technology behind it?

A new model is emerging in the industry analyst world, which is perhaps the closest commercial model to the academic research world. The analyst model was originally created in the 1990s to help companies sort through myriad new technologies on the market to determine which would be the best for their respective businesses. Over time, as the technology choices and options became clearer, often through industry consolidation, consumers of analyst research began looking more for help with how to use the technology, how to solve various business problems, as opposed to what to buy. Through it all, access to research was limited, to clients of the firm or to those willing to pay a very hefty price tag. Even today, many research firms charge a price tag for clients and others to share the research with their business partners, customers, even their employees—the parties upon whom they will become increasingly dependent for collective problem solving.

Former Gartner and AMR analyst Lora Cecere hopes to disrupt the model. One of the world's foremost supply-chain experts, Lora recently launched a new analyst firm where the majority of her industry research will be free for the taking. In fact, she wants as many people as possible to use it and share it. Instead of a revenue stream, Lora sees research as a marketing tool. "When people read the research, I believe they will want to do business with me," says Lora. Lora's firm has also launched what she calls the supply-chain insights community (www.supplychaininsights.com), an online platform where she not only publishes her research for free, but also openly encourages others to post their work product and create their own collaborative communities. The only requirement is that the material is designed to advance the supply-chain discipline, rather than being blatantly commercial. As Lora explains it, "As a single entity, my firm cannot figure it all out, but with a community, we can bring the experts together to develop new insights through our collective knowledge."

Compounding the problem as it relates to leadership development is that educational methodologies have also not changed to a large extent in decades, if not centuries. Most students still sit in classrooms (whether physical or online) while the professor or teacher transmits knowledge. That's part of the problem. Even the move to more mobile learning environments has not changed the paradigm. While people can access learning from anywhere in the world, which delivers real value to those whose access to education was limited by distance, the approach is still largely the same. We have not fundamentally changed the model, just the delivery method. Too much of what we are doing with online education is just an online version of what we were doing in the classroom. We need to get rid of the existing model before we apply the technology.

The primarily instructor-led learning model creates yet another problem. The instructor is considered the expert, and many of them are quite knowledgeable about the subject at hand. But do they question what they know? As U.S. President Harry Truman once said, an expert is "afraid to learn anything new because he wouldn't be an expert anymore." It's an oversimplification, but in many cases, instructors will stick with the subject matter they are most comfortable with and pass on their view of the world. And if they do their jobs as intended, they can replicate the expert scenario in their students, who now become the experts and are predisposed to a certain way of thinking: what they have learned, as opposed to what they don't know. After all, they committed a large amount of time and resources to get there. This precludes the opportunity to look at a problem from a different perspective. The same old way of thinking is reinforced, which is not what is needed in today's business environment.

If you think about it, the instructor at the head of the class is not unlike the now outdated hierarchical business model, with the leader at the top whose primary responsibility was keeping things under control and moving efficiently. As long as you had a succession plan and focused your leadership development efforts on those in the pipeline, you were in good shape. Leadership development programs were focused on individual leaders, not the leadership capabilities of the organization itself.

Our system of rewards followed suit. Do a good job, get a gold star; and in the end, the one with the most gold stars wins. The forced ranking performance review systems used by so many companies serve as a barrier to taking a broader organizational approach to developing leadership. It sets up a competition among individuals, as opposed to creating an environment that fosters collaboration, which is critical to innovation at all levels.

Performance measurement systems are also outdated, with employees evaluated based on their ability to meet a specific set of quantifiable goals and time-based deliverables. If you do this many things in this amount of time, you get this grade. The model worked quite well when outcomes were more predictable and success was more clearly defined and considered on an individual basis. But in an uncertain global market, how can you ever be certain that you have settled on the right goals and that doing this, this many times, will give you the results you want? People and teams should be evaluated on their ability to solve problems, not on how many tasks they perform.

Broaden the Focus

As it is typically practiced, leadership development does not develop leadership. We need to change our approach from a focus on the individual to one that strives to develop a robust leadership system across the organization—from the core to the edge. The results of the 2013 Conference Board CEO Challenge signal that global CEOs are beginning to recognize this need. As noted earlier, human capital was listed as the number one challenge globally for organizations, significantly higher than its seventh ranking just a year before. Perhaps more interestingly is how CEOs plan to tackle this challenge, with the strategies focused more on growing and retaining existing talent and raising employee engagement. As the 2013 report notes, "This indicates a shift toward overall organizational capability building and away from a narrower approach that emphasizes individual high-potential talent" (Mitchell, Ray, and van Ark, 2013).

Given the magnitude and breadth of the challenge, CEOs need to ensure that strategic talent management is part of their executive level strategic plan. And those in charge of talent management for their companies need to understand the business and the global environment as well as the CEOs they are supporting. If not, talent management leaders can be little more than a glorified concierge service, and we have already discussed in painful detail the challenges of outsourcing leadership development. It's up to the CEO to raise the stature of HR beyond just a compensation-planning engine and make talent management a strategic business imperative. It is incumbent upon HR and talent management to live up to the assignment by building a leadership system that supports the overall corporate strategy and aligns with objectives around business models, organizational structure, and culture. Perhaps more importantly, leadership systems must align with what I call *extreme performance* management. As described in another book published by ASTD Press, *The Executive Guide to Integrated Talent Management*, extreme performance is achieved "when leaders can create organizations that will be profitable and grow simultaneously in markets as diverse as India, China, North America, and Europe" (Neal and Kovach, 2010). Extreme performance can be incredibly powerful, but it is only possible when leadership development is successfully managed in a holistic manner across an organization, not in individual silos.

Individual thinking is one of the biggest pitfalls for executives and hiring managers. When looking for candidates, they run the risk of focusing too much on the specifications for a particular job, as opposed to the needs of the entire organization. They consider if the candidates fit a specific job, not whether they fit the organization. For example, you might find the perfect person to lead your cloud-computing initiatives based on her technical experience, but does that candidate also know how to lead an organization, to scale capabilities, to think beyond the specific tasks at hand in order to discover new ways to deliver sustained value to the organization, and to effectively share that vision with others?

Consider the work being done to upgrade GE's leadership competency model, which many consider to be one of the world's premier corporate-led programs. GE Chairman and CEO Jeffrey Immelt takes an active role in talent management and is the catalyst behind revamping the program to foster what his CLO and VP of executive development Susan Peters describes as "the attributes of…the '21st Century Leader'—a leader who can thrive in a global economy that's in constant flux" (McIlvaine, 2010).

Peters says Immelt believes 21st-century thinkers must be systems thinkers. I would argue that those responsible for talent management strategies must be system thinkers as well. In order to develop leaders—which I see as an individual intervention— while also developing the company's leadership capability, which requires a more organization-wide approach, leaders need to design an end-to-end system that achieves results at both the macro and micro levels. The failure of many talent management executives is that they focus on developing leaders without addressing the overall dynamics of the system. They focus narrowly on identifying leaders to develop and running them through a set suite of programs. In the absence of strong organizational leadership, these newly developed leaders can find themselves in an environment where they cannot fulfill their potential and may be looking for other opportunities. In other words, non-systems thinking can lead to a situation where you are simply building great leaders who leave your organization to go to work for your competitors.

Designing the end-to-end system first requires knowing what the organization requires to achieve its objectives. Talent executives need to understand what globalisation will mean to their business in terms of competition and varied customer needs, and what it means to employees in terms of what will enable them to deliver the quality of work needed and what will keep them engaged. As with everything we have discussed around the increasingly global nature of work, it depends. What an employee in Palo Alto wants or needs is different from her counterpart in Bangalore. The same is true for your customers and your business partners.

Let's start with innovation, which, as we explored earlier, is critical across the organization. Innovation rarely comes from the top of the organization, but it is the top executive's responsibility to create a culture that fosters innovation. It's also the executive's responsibility to ensure an effective leadership development program is in place to teach the organization how to experiment so that innovation can flourish. All of this requires an environment where leaders and followers are asking different questions to come to different conclusions. They need to think differently, and to think differently, they need to learn differently. Different does not happen in the classroom setting. It happens in the context of the markets they are trying to serve. And it's more about *doing* in those contexts, not just learning. As Western Union CEO Hikmet Ersek explains: "Millions of people wanted to give me advice. I took their advice and I looked at business schools, books, and consultants. But it was on the road and in the markets the business serves that I learned the true lessons of global leadership."

That's why I am excited about what's happening with Harvard's new FIELD program. Warren Bennis talked about the changes being made at the venerable Boston-based institution in a

BusinessWeek blog, congratulating Nitin Nohria, the current dean of the business school, for recognizing that "To make more progress in the education of leaders, we have to get better at translating knowing into doing" (Bennis, 2012). Another important point called out by Warren is that students who do not do well in the FIELD move to what is referred to as the "failed track," where they "focus on what went wrong and why." It's not a failing grade; it's a learning opportunity. And here's where those of us in the real world can learn from the business schools, because while many companies have the best of intentions to learn from failure, few actually devote the time to do it well.

We are all a bit hypocritical in this respect. Academia's views on failure are contradictory. Admissions officers recognize that people learn from failure, but their job is not usually to admit people who have failed. This is the kind of thinking behind the institutions we turn to develop our current and emerging leaders. No wonder folks like Steve Jobs, Bill Gates, and Mark Zuckerberg opted to drop out.

It is the talent management executive's responsibility to make sure leaders are rewarded, not penalized, for taking risks. Employees need permission to try out a new idea, to fail a few times, to assess the dynamics around the failures, and to try again (sometimes yet again) before succeeding. In the process, employees and organizations should continue to re-evaluate objectives and goals to see if they should be reset based on the lessons learned. Innovation and goal setting also require employees to have a clear line of sight into corporate strategy. How does an employee's work help the organization create more value in the market? They must understand the meaning behind their work in order to be inspired and motivated.

The most innovative employees want to align with other innovators and with their communities of practice, rendering employee engagement programs obsolete that depend on loyalty to a corporation. How does this factor in to your overall talent management and performance measurement systems? Engagement comes from meaningful work with meaningful colleagues—that translates into meaning for a company, for an industry, and for society at large.

When things are working at an optimal level, rewards and inspiration come from within. It's not unlike the philosophy behind the Montessori method of education, which is designed to foster a child's innate passion for learning and natural tendency to work. Children are given the opportunity to help shape their work and have more control over their environment. Two of the most innovative global leaders today—Google founders Larry Page and Sergey Brin—were both Montessori kids. One of our most successful programs at Cisco—the Executive Action Learning Forum, highlighted later in this chapter—leveraged the Montessori model for adult learning.

Once talent management leaders understand the overall business and what is critical for success now and in the future, only then can they develop meaningful measurements for their work. They must be derived out of the context of the world in which the business is operating, just as meaningful business performance data is drawn out of the market. But they don't need to go it alone, nor should they. Instead of the more typical approach—where HR professionals develop performance management systems in a vacuum and simply ask for executive blessing—I advise them to engage business leaders early on.

EXECUTIVES TAKE CHARGE

CEOs should do the same. Seek out your talent executives. Bring them into your inner circle. Make them partners, just like your CFO,

COO, and legal counsel. Then, work with them to develop discipline around your leadership and performance measurement systems to the same degree that you evaluate the rest of your business assets. How many times have you heard a company claim that people are its biggest asset? But rarely do you see companies manage talent with the same kind of *strategic* analytical rigor that they use to manage their business investments. Do you really know which members of your talent portfolio are growing value and which are diluting it? At Cisco, we did the math and determined the cost of having low capacity people in critical leadership positions—in hard dollars based on a multiplier against cash compensation—and then translated these numbers into cents per share. Computing these kinds of calculations for your leadership portfolio will certainly get your attention, and the attention of your board.

Once your leadership system is built, don't forget about it. Just as executives need to continually deconstruct and reconstruct their organizational and business models, so, too, do those in charge of leadership development. Sustained success requires continual re-creation to ensure you are delivering value, whether it's to the market or to the organization.

When it comes to measuring the performance of your leadership development strategy and programs, as opposed to the overall performance of your talent, the Conference Board CEO Challenge report found a point of contention between the CEOs and those responsible for leading talent management in their organizations. The CEOs ranked "requiring the use of analytics to articulate the business impact of key human capital initiatives and programs" last among the strategies presented to undertake in response to their concerns about human capital. The report says human capital professionals regard such analytics as a critical factor in helping their function contribute to business success. I actually agree with the CEOs on this one. Taking a decidedly analytical approach is critically important. But to be relevant to the CEO, human capital measures must make the connection between leadership talent and predictions of business growth, innovation, and productivity.

The problem with traditional measurements around human capital data is that they are lagging, not leading, and are rarely predictive indicators. It's not good enough to look just at how many high potential people you have in a particular job and your retention rate. As we have already discussed, the systems of evaluating people are broken, but we continue to collect data around them. Instead of measuring and reporting retention numbers, or how many executives you ran through this program or that, take a look at what's happening in the market. Which organizations are you hiring your leaders from? Do you have the kind of leadership brand that helps you attract the right capabilities? If you have a huge innovation platform and are only hiring from traditional companies, will that get you where you need to be? Who is leaving the company and where are they going? If your people are going to more interesting, more innovative competitors, what is it that those companies do that is drawing the kind of talent you want?

Finally, consider how you are evaluating individual performers within the context of a more collective approach. You still have people who need feedback and a system of rewards that helps drive the behaviors needed. The gold stars aren't going away, not completely, but the actions and accomplishments that warrant recognition should take into account competencies and accomplishments related to collaboration, knowledge sharing and, of course, team and overall organizational performance. I suggest you also take into account how your employees work with others within your ecosystem and how well your partners are performing. In many cases, their performance is dependent upon you, and yours on them. It is, after all, a great big connected world in which we are leading.

But how do you take these concepts and put them into action? As I have said before, the one-to-many model does not work when developing leadership. Your approach must be customized to the needs of your organization. But I can share some specific examples of programs that I believe exemplify this approach. The following four company case studies showcase the approaches outlined in this chapter.

Cisco Systems: Executive Action Learning Forum

Cisco Systems' *Executive Action Learning Forum* (E-ALF) was designed in collaboration with Marthin DeBeer, who at the time was Cisco's chief innovation officer, to achieve two objectives simultaneously: to develop top talent, while driving strategic innovation. Launched in 2007, the program gave high-potential leaders an opportunity to strengthen specific strategic management, team development, and general management skills in what Cisco called a viability lab, as opposed to a classroom or simulated setting free of the risks of a complex business environment. Participants were presented with high-profile business opportunities and given the chance to apply for funding for ideas that they developed during the 16-week program. In the process, Cisco was able to test the viability of both the business proposals as well as the future leaders who would be responsible for bringing new ideas to market.

Held twice a year, E-ALF was open to 60 high-potential employees by invitation only. Each employee had to go through a rigorous assessment to identify his strengths as well as areas for improvement. Next, the group received instruction on business strategy and operations from Cisco's top executives and MIT faculty. The bulk of the practical experience occurred over a 10-week period, during which employees were separated into teams ranging from six to 10 members who compete against each other to launch a new business product or opportunity that is strategic to Cisco's business. To qualify for E-ALF, each project had to represent a $1 billion-plus opportunity for Cisco.

Each team represented a diverse group that crosses every conceivable line—function, generation, geography, and gender. They were all considered among the best and the brightest in their respective areas. That said, Cisco instructed the teams to work together in collaborative fashion, as opposed to following traditional hierarchical reporting relationships. Distinguished engineers, for example, and top salespeople interacted on a level playing field. Each team received guidance from business advisors and subject matter experts who became virtual team members; in addition, each participant was assigned a personal management consultant from the Cisco Center for Collaborative Leadership (C3) to help accelerate individual leadership development. C3 provided team and leadership feedback to ensure that participants were developing specific skills.

In support of Cisco's globalisation efforts, teams involved in an E-ALF cohort focused on emerging markets travelled to India and China, as well as received advice and input from people with deep expertise in those regions. Eighty percent of the participants had never been to China or India before participating in E-ALF. With growth in emerging markets a strategic objective for Cisco, this program helped broaden the perspective of prospective company leaders who could be called on to support future initiatives. One of the team members noted that the experience introduced him to the complexity of working within an emerging market, as compared to doing business with the U.S. government. The advice he received was that he would have to expand his perspectives to be considered for advancement. Cisco, meanwhile, gained additional value from the work product of the emerging market teams, which developed various ideas that Cisco subsequently launched as part of its emerging markets strategy.

At the end of the program, a governance board tested the viability of each team's idea and decided whether it was worth funding. Essentially an internal venture capital committee, the board evaluated and graded each team against a rigorous set of criteria. In some cases, they asked teams whose plans proved viable to lead the initiatives going forward.

Although E-ALF cost between $12-15,000 per employee, Cisco's return-on-investment came when a team project was launched in the market, as well as when participants applied their learning to drive innovation through better collaboration, to understand competitive markets and strategic planning, and to create high-performing teams. E-ALF was named "Most Innovative Talent Management Program Initiative" by the International Quality and Productivity Center.

Within 5 years of its formation, E-ALF teams had generated more than $25 billion of what Cisco's chief innovation officer called "proposed value creation." One idea proposed during a forum that Cisco went on to develop, the Smart Grid, revamps energy grids to make them faster and more cost effective.

There have also been impressive gains for the people involved as well. At the time this case study was written, 20 percent of the participants had been promoted. And, since the forums began, Cisco has lost only two percent of the high-potential employees who've attended E-ALF. That rate reflects the value that high performers place on developmental opportunities. In fact, E-ALF has been an engagement and acceleration tool for the company.

Although participants are not rewarded financially, they are engaged by the intellectual challenge that comes with tackling relevant real-world problems, the internal recognition that comes with being selected, and the enhanced skills that fuel their career advancement. Another powerful motivator is the knowledge that, as an employee and stakeholder in Cisco's future, each participant has an opportunity to make a significant contribution to the company's success.

Starwood Hotels & Resorts Worldwide Inc.: Leadership 100

Starwood Hotels and Resorts executive development program reflects the unique leadership style of CEO Frits van Paasschen. Known for his accomplishments with leading global brands, Frits recognizes that real firepower behind brands rests on being able to create a collective, global mindset for the organization. Case in point: In the midst of the global financial crisis, when many companies were scaling back on leadership development, Frits did just the opposite. In 2008, in the depths of the worst hotel/lodging recession since the Great Depression, he chose to invest in leaders by building a tightly aligned cadre of top leaders from around the world and launched an executive development initiative called Starwood Leadership 100.

A move like this reflects Frits's innovative management approach. He believes that Starwood can cultivate a more global culture by understanding, appreciating, and leveraging diverse societal perspectives and approaches to managing the business. Having lived and worked around the world, Frits values global diversity, and believes that ongoing open and direct communication across languages and cultures is key to Starwood's success in a fast-changing world.

Frits's entire leadership team, along with their direct reports, makes up Starwood Leadership 100. The concept is to bring the company's top leaders together to discuss and interpret what's happening in the world and the implications and opportunities for Starwood. With more than 1100 hotels in nearly 100 countries, Starwood enjoys being the most global hotel company, and this gives Frits and his top team a unique vantage point to globalisation—or as Frits says, "courtside seats to the global economy." At the core of the Leadership 100 initiative is the philosophy that the company is smarter and more agile when it taps into the unique perspective of diverse leaders and aligns around common goals.

Since 2008, Starwood has held five Leadership 100 gatherings. The locations are carefully selected as places that epitomize globalisation and the rapid change in the world through rising wealth and digital technology—cities like Beijing and Dubai. Frits believes that leaders learn more by having a shared experience in a vastly different environment from their normal day-to-day, and as such the Leadership 100 conferences are intentionally designed to foster a vastly different way of thinking. With the backdrop of these global cities, Starwood's leaders engage in a way that embeds a more global mindset. All elements of the meeting agenda are thoughtfully designed to spur the company's strategy for global growth.

Frits is more than a symbolic leader of these gatherings. He uses the Starwood Leadership 100 conference as an opportunity to share his own thinking about the world at large. His worldview is shaped by seeing "beyond the headlines to the trend lines," and the Leadership 100 forum gives him a chance to sit down with his top leaders and have meaningful discussions. He takes them through his very deliberate and continual thought process. Frits is continually reshaping his thinking: synthesizing information, making adjustments as appropriate, and communicating to make his thought process accessible to others. Just as importantly, he takes the time to listen: to find out what others are thinking, to gauge how his vision resonates with the group, and to create a shared perspective. This level of understanding also helps increase adoption. As Frits explains it, "I can be very powerful with my message, but if we can get the entire leadership team believing and saying the same thing, we are 100 times as powerful."

Red Hat: Leadership the Red Hat Way

Red Hat, the predominant global player in open source software, approaches leadership development in much the same way as it develops software: in an open and collaborative fashion. With an appreciation that leadership across the organization is a differentiator for the company, Red Hat set out to uncover what it means to lead "the Red Hat way"—the specific qualities that create a leader who sees the impact of her efforts multiply within the organization.

The initial discovery phase was a multiyear effort, because like everything Red Hat does, this is an ongoing, iterative process. Rather than focus on what needs to change and what's not working, Red Hat used an appreciative inquiry approach, asking employees: "When we are at our very best, what are we doing exceptionally well? Of those things, what do other companies also do when they are at their best, and what is it that we do that sets us apart? Ultimately, what makes Red Hat different and great?"

But Red Hat did not ask this question once or in just one way. Those responsible for the leadership brand asked the question again, and again, in workshops and focus groups. Employees were encouraged to provide lots of detail and descriptors: how "good" looks, feels, even sounds, with as much drama and dialogue as possible.

By sifting through data (which continue to be collected), the company was able to identify five themes that appeared to be common to employees around the globe. Those themes were then shared with the global leadership team to make sure nothing was missing or askew. Nothing was, which is further testament to the company's strong alignment vertically, horizontally, and internationally.

The five themes that define Red Hat's unique leadership brand are:

- **Connection**—People thrive when they are part of a community connected by their ideas and passions.

- **Transparency**—People grow and learn by sharing, not withholding, information.
- **Meritocracy**—The best ideas win. Respect is earned by making visible contributions, rather than just by title or rank.
- **Collaboration**—People are given the opportunity to offer ideas and feedback to both peers and leaders.
- **Trust**—These traits lay the foundation for leading the Red Hat way, but people must also trust that a leader has their best interests at heart.

But Red Hat doesn't look at these attributes in silos. There is a complementary nature as well as an element of balance—not too much, not too little—to the qualities, and when that balance is reached, greatness happens. Red Hat defines these leadership qualities in its competency model, providing employees with a great deal of detail about what it takes to be successful at the company. In turn, the company learns a great deal about why people come to Red Hat and more importantly, why they stay.

For CEO Jim Whitehurst, sustaining Red Hat's unique culture, as defined and supported by its leadership brand, is core to the company's growth strategy. Over the past decade, Red Hat has been on an explosive trajectory, becoming the first open source software development company to reach $1 billion in annual revenue. Just a decade ago, the company was focused almost singularly on gaining traction in the enterprise server market. Today, the company offers a full suite of enterprise infrastructure software, competing with industry giants like Oracle and Microsoft. For many companies, that kind of growth can lead to either complacency or a desire to be like the big boys. But not Red Hat. Sustaining the culture and leadership brand takes on even more importance as the company grows its capabilities, with more complex products and a larger global footprint. And the leadership qualities defined in Red Hat's competency model will continue to evolve with it, thanks to a senior leadership team and a talent development organization that knows how to listen and learn.

Western Union: Western Union University

Like many large corporations, Western Union has long offered an in-house training program, which it dubs Western Union University (WUU). The development programs within the University, in and of themselves, are not necessarily hugely unique. What is unique and, as a result, incredibly powerful, is the vested interest that Hikmet Ersek has taken in WUU since becoming CEO. He sees it as playing an integral part in reinventing the financial services giant.

GE-trained, Hikmet brings a very deliberate approach to leadership development at Western Union, something the company had previously lacked. He views talent and training as he would any other aspect of his overall strategic plan. The fundamental questions are: What is the objective? What do we need to do to get there? What assets do we have and how can we leverage them? What additional investments or changes do we need to make? What are the results we can expect if we follow the plan?

Hikmet leverages his entire leadership team in the process. His direct reports serve not only as teachers but also to ensure that the subject matter and methodology are tied directly to company objectives and are aligned with the evolving corporate brand and marketplace. Over the course of six months, top performing managers and directors from different countries work together on priority projects for specific regions. Starting with prototypes, the teams refine their solutions by connecting with key stakeholders, breaking down organizational and functional silos, and increasing collaboration in order to drive change. At the conclusion, the student teams present their results to regional leadership, a process that helps develop their executive presentation skills and helps advance their ideas and their leadership potential. Here are two examples:

Western Union Business Solutions (WUBS) Customer Service Delivery Framework

This team's objective was to enhance customer service for WU's business-to-business division by creating a delivery framework that would increase understanding and define ownership of operational processes. The team reviewed the current payment-processing life cycle and defined and aligned service-level agreements between the various stakeholders. A detailed train-the-trainer model allows knowledge sharing in a standardized way, which in turn enables employees to perform operations that achieve both time and quality goals. By applying these improved processes to just two specific customer segments, the team's business case estimated an additional value of $2.4 million to WUBS in the first year alone.

Staged Transactions

Staged Transactions is a phrase that had previously only been used internally to describe an alternative transactions process between WU agents and customers. Introducing the term externally—and more importantly the concept—was designed to improve the customer experience by reducing various pain points along the path of purchase. For example, customers can use a web or mobile device from anywhere (for example, their home or office) to prepopulate data about how and when they want to send money. This minimizes time spent at the physical WU locations and reduces errors associated with manual data entry by the agent. By handling their own data, customers can increase privacy and overcome language barriers at the point of service. In addition to defining the value proposition for both customers and agents, the team developed both a marketing plan to reach a newly identified target audience and a phased, nationwide launch plan. The team estimated the first-year value of the project to be $4 million as a result of revenue from customer acquisition and retention and reduced operational expenses through faster process times and potentially lower agent-labor costs.

A key component of Hikmet's strategy is changing how Western Union has been typically viewed—from a consumer-to-consumer wire transfer company to the premier financial services organization for the under-served and under-banked. But changing how the world views Western

Union also requires changing how his employees view the organization. That can take them out of their comfort zones. After all, Western Union has a long-established brand and presence in the marketplace, one that has served the company well. But helping people become comfortable with the uncomfortable is part of Hikmet's unique leadership style. He is not just trying to change a business model; he is working to change the culture.

Given the close connection between corporate culture and what employees believe and how they behave, Hikmet believes there are five behaviors employees need to exhibit to transform the company. Through WUU, he is leveraging the power of learning to help employees

- Be inspired.
- Get connected.
- Take responsibility.
- Be driven.
- Change the game.

These behaviors are integrated into another WUU signature program: the behavior workshops. Here, the learning process is more exploratory and conversational, with two- to three-hour dialogues focused on why each of these behaviors supports what Western Union is trying to accomplish in specific geographic markets. By completing a set of action-planning worksheets, graduates can translate the dialogues into specific actions they can practice on the job.

With each of these programs, Hikmet has ensured that leadership development is part of the overall corporate strategic plan. More importantly, he has assumed responsibility, in much the same way as he assumes responsibility for other initiatives critical to the company's long-term viability.

You can read more about each of the executives who led these best practices in the profiles in section IV of the book.

CHAPTER 7

Raising Global Leaders

In the prior chapters, I've discussed what is required to lead in today's complex global environment. I've questioned the predominant approach to leadership development. And I have challenged executives to take charge of their business's most vital asset: their people. But now I want to focus on something even more important: how we raise the next generation of global leaders. This is where I get very personal. How do you instill the 10 essential traits in your children, such that they will be best prepared to take their positions as global citizens and leaders? The beauty of the essential traits is that they are not exclusive to business. They are elemental to anyone who intends to lead, whether in the corporate world, in public service, or as catalysts for social change or cultural advancement. I spent a lot of time earlier discussing the essential traits because they are so important to develop in yourself as you seek to lead your business, and as you work to instill those qualities across your organization and the broader ecosystems within which you operate.

A common theme among many of the exceptional global leaders with whom I have worked is a desire to leave a legacy that includes making a positive change in the world. For those who are parents, this includes preparing their children for the future they will soon inherit. It's a future that will be hard to predict—remember

VUCA (volatile, uncertain, complex, and ambiguous)? But there is also beauty in that world, with different cultures to explore and people to engage, new possibilities to discover that have yet to be considered, and opportunities for our children to create legacies of their own. What grander goal can we have than to prepare our children to enter that world wide-eyed, aware, and ready? There are resources available to help you, but just like leadership in the business world, this is not something you can outsource. Just like leadership in the business world, I believe it is your ultimate responsibility to do this right, certainly in your own family. I would also call on you to work by helping improve the systems in which our children are taught, but unfortunately not always fully educated (at least not in the broad respect that the world demands).

I told you it was personal, but also extremely important. Your children depend upon your performance in this area. It can be intimidating for even the most successful global leaders. But it can also be extremely rewarding, and perhaps some of the most fun you will have in years.

Let's start with the essential traits. Think of what they offer children:

- A Strong Sense of Self—Having the strength of conviction to move forward with courage and determination.

- Multimodal Thinking—The ability to rapidly absorb, synthesize, organize, and most importantly, make sense of the world around them.

- An Experimental Mind and the Freedom to Fail Fast—A willingness to try new things and to learn quickly, rather than be set back by their mistakes.

- Constructive Collaboration—The ability to create something bigger and better by working well with others.

- Empathy—Having the kinds of insights that only come through deep understanding of what others are experiencing.

These traits are addressed in countless child-rearing books and parenting classes. Having been clinically trained as a child psychologist, I have studied these topics extensively. What I want to do is share some of my clinical knowledge in the context of raising global leaders. By understanding how children develop, you can better identify where they are in the maturation cycle and, in turn, what you can expect from them, what you can teach them, and what you should be watching for along the way.

There are real advantages to sensitizing our children to a much larger world early in life. Many of those interviewed for this book talked about how developing the next generation of leaders really begins in the home, by exposing them in an appropriate manner to the world around them and creating learning opportunities around world issues.

We can learn a lot from the way many of the executives profiled in section IV are raising their own children. They take a different approach than most because they are so much more in tune to the dynamics of leading and living in the whole of the world, as opposed to seeing the world from a single vantage point that can conceal the wonder, and at times the tragedy, of what life is really like.

ONE CHILD'S PERSPECTIVE

An executive colleague of mine's daughter, Ainsley, has spent the last four years of her young life abroad, moving from her Colorado home when her father was placed on an expat assignment in Bangalore, India and then Singapore. She has attended third, fourth, and fifth grades in international schools and, at just 11 years old, has a worldly perspective that is missing in many adults. More importantly, she is already exhibiting many of the essential traits that will provide a strong foundation for her as she matures into a young woman and I suspect a highly accomplished adult. She and the rest of the world will be better off for it.

Ainsley speaks about how her experiences have opened her eyes to what is going on in a world that she didn't know about and did not realize she needed to understand. She was particularly struck by the slums in India. It was two years ago when she first saw them, but she still talks about the experience vividly. She was particularly stunned by how many people in the world struggle to get clean drinking water. "We're wasting water in the U.S. We let it run and run when we are taking showers. I want to let people know that they need to change their behavior," she states emphatically. Rather than being overwhelmed by these conditions or disheartened by the waste, Ainsley wants to change the world.

Ainsley also takes great joy in discovering the world, with the natural curiosity of a child but also in a manner that I suspect will stay with her and serve her well all her life. She cannot wait to tell all her friends about her experiences, the good and the bad: the beautiful beaches in Thailand and the Maldives, as well as the demoralizing killing fields in Cambodia and the jails in Vietnam. Even at this young age, she reflects on "what the world has done to people."

She wants her friends to learn more, too, even if they do not have the opportunity to experience the broader world firsthand. She wants them to join her in watching *CNN for Kids*, a program that broadcasts international news geared for a younger audience. As they learn, she hopes they will remain open-minded and stop, look, listen, even feel, before making judgments. Her other words of advice: try new things, like different foods "even if some taste really, really terrible," and try to see the good in things ("even when they seem bad").

Where does this young person go from here? She will keep experiencing, experimenting, building on what is already a strong sense of self, and, if she gets a chance, she wants to go to Italy and eat some real Italian ice cream, too!

THE GLOBAL LEADER'S PERSPECTIVE

Truly global leaders know what it takes—for an individual, a company, even a nation—to be competitive today. From a parenting perspective, this often translates into a question: How do I teach my child(ren) to be comfortable and competent in what Frits from Starwood would call "this great age of change"?

It is no longer enough for children to have the proper reading, writing, and arithmetic skills. They need to learn critical thinking skills, to see the possibilities, to continually adapt to a world in which creativity is the value differentiator and agile is the new smart. Our future leaders will need to navigate the world with a greater sense of self-confidence and courage than ever before. Childhood is a perfect time to start guiding them, as children are naturally curious about the world around them. Take that curiosity and teach them how to become world-class explorers. Help them experiment to see what happens if they do this, or how things change if they do things differently. Let them—better yet, encourage them to—question norms and challenge structures that can limit thinking and innovation. It is our job as parents to provide our children with safe boundaries, but with lots of room for experimentation and, yes, failure. Then, help them learn from their mistakes. Think how much better it is for them to learn these skills now, as opposed to when they are older. Without these important early lessons, they may grow up afraid to take risks for fear of failure or become paralyzed rather than better informed when they do fail. Help them develop a deep sense of empathy that allows them to flourish in a world of differences, of diversity, and of continual change. By understanding others, they are better prepared to create greater value in the world, not just what's best for them. The irony is, by creating value for others, they will eventually create more value for themselves. By learning how to live well with others, they can multiply that value, by building upon a collective versus singular mind and prosper in both their personal and professional lives. Grand goals, I know, but achievable, especially if you understand a bit more about how children develop.

A CHILD PSYCHOLOGIST'S PERSPECTIVE

Child development begins with a sense of security and predictability about the world around them. Is the world a safe place? When I am hungry, will there be someone to feed me? If I am scared, will someone comfort and protect me? This stage of development, which begins at birth, is critically important as it sets the stage for how children formulate their view of the world: Is it frightening or a grand place for adventure? Certainly, life events can shake this viewpoint, but a strong foundation increases the likelihood of being able to survive even the most challenging of times.

As children mature, they begin exploring cause and effect. This is a particularly enjoyable time, for children and parents. They make a silly face and someone reacts. They giggle and make the face again, much to their parents' delight. They build blocks and knock them down. Mom lights a birthday candle; the child blows it out. They will continue to test cause and effect into adolescence. Granted, it might not be as much fun, but it is vital to development.

How we react to our children's behavior—what we encourage, what we discourage—has long-lasting impacts.

I remember one Christmas when my son Tucker was just three years old, and he wanted to keep all of the Christmas decorations at the bottom of the tree where he could see them. We went through the entire holiday season with one of the more awkwardly decorated trees, but to this day, he remembers that experience and that encouragement to try something different. Many years later, he asked if we could have a Jewish Christmas tree. At first I tried explaining that Jewish people did not celebrate Christmas and likely did not have Christmas trees, but that point went past him, and I discovered what he really wanted—to explore new religions. So, we decorated the tree with blue and silver and celebrated for eight nights, talking about Hanukkah, reading about the customs, and making and enjoying traditional foods. If I had discouraged Tucker when he was three, he might have not have felt he had permission to explore those new things that intrigued him.

Another critical quality is empathy, that, as a clinician, I believe develops early in life, but only if a child learns to moderate his narcissism. Remember, narcissism is something we all have; it's just whether it is the productive or the unhealthy kind. If children grow up with a sense of entitlement, they may learn intellectually what it means to be empathetic, but it will never be part of who they are. Empathy forms in a meaningful way when children begin to understand that there are others in the world who may have the same, or more importantly, different perspectives and needs. They begin to understand there is grey in the world, that people, including themselves, aren't completely good or completely bad, but often a fascinating mixture of both. It's also the beginning of learning to live with ambiguity, which is fundamental to so many of the essential traits.

Empathy lays the groundwork for more productive interpersonal relationships, and as children mature in this manner, their choice of play will shift as well. Children explore their worlds through play. As a psychologist, I have always found how children play—the games they choose, the rules they follow (or don't), the skills they are mastering (or trying to), and the ways they include others (individually or on teams)—is symbolic of how they are learning at various stages of their development.

Watch how your children play: how they win or lose, when they choose to collaborate or compete, if they can be counted on or can count on their teammates. Through games, children first learn the social norms (the rules for this game) and then the consequences of their actions on themselves and others. Here is where I have significant concerns about the highly violent content of some of today's video games. There are many video games that create opportunities for children to learn about the world and develop skills and appreciation, some of which we will discuss later. But games that foster violence early on, especially without demonstrating the human and social implications of that violence, can be highly detrimental to developing empathetic insights and relationships.

Insight develops along a continuum, beginning with cause and effect. True insight—into how your actions affect others and how your own emotions affect you personally—develops in conjunction with empathy and your ability to form interpersonal relationships. To be truly insightful, you need a balance of understanding how you move through the world *and* how others move in relationship to you. It's that dynamic nature of *you plus others* that creates insight. Only being insightful about yourself can be unproductively narcissistic. But equally, if you are only insightful about others, you may fail to recognize how what they do affects others, including yourself. It's a delicate balance, and as a result, I believe some people have very little insight. No matter how hard they try, they just don't get it. Sometimes they are too self-absorbed, but other times their parents may have failed to foster those opportunities to help them gain insight.

I recently worked with Liz Gasper, a highly successful start-up CFO who described how her father would ask her every night at dinner what she learned that day. Then he would explore further, asking thought-provoking questions about all the things that she had told him. She's nearly 60 now and still vividly remembers those conversations, and the role they played in developing the person she is and also how she continues to learn from life's experiences.

With a better understanding of how children mature, here are five areas to explore with your children, along with advice from some of the global leaders you have already met in this book. And, you know me by now, I will also offer a few suggestions for challenging and changing the systems in which children are raised.

1. Parents Without Borders

A common theme that comes up in many of the in-depth discussions I have with global leaders is how to teach children to be active participants in the world, as opposed to spectators. Being a global leader is a team sport, and it is up to us to help our children get in the game, not sit on the sidelines. They need to learn how to play various roles, from trusted teammate to captain.

To fully participate in the world, as a player and a leader, children must be open and receptive to experiencing the world as it really is, not some protected version. If you have the opportunity to travel internationally with your children—something most executives highly encourage—don't keep them isolated in an all-inclusive resort or gated community. Even if you choose to stay at one of the many wonderful properties around the world, take your children out, explore the local communities where people live and work, engage in conversations, and try the local cuisine.

Both Wim Elfrink and Hikmet Ersek speak enthusiastically about taking their sons with them on business trips for the very deliberate purpose of introducing them to various different cultures. When Wim first took his son to India, the young boy's first reaction was to focus on the differences: the people spoke and dressed differently, and with some degree of apprehension, he commented that they must be poor because some wore no shoes. Rather than chastise his son, Wim engaged him in a dialogue, helping him focus less on what he was seeing and more on what he wasn't. By creating opportunities for his son to not just look and react, but rather to experience firsthand how other people live and work, Wim helped the young boy explore the reasons behind the differences. This is the beginning of what it takes to create empathy.

Wim's initiative to teach his son empathy at a young age is supported by psychological and developmental research that indicates empathy can be a learned trait. As Daniel Goleman, a fellow psychologist who focuses much of his research on emotional intelligence, wrote in the *Harvard Business Review* article, "What Makes a Leader?" (2004), empathy begins in the brain's limbic system, which regulates emotion and memory, not in the neocortex, where we do most of our analytical thinking. In other words, empathy can be developed as a result of life's experiences.

As a middle-schooler, Wim's son would not be expected to have mastered the art of empathy, but with the experiences Wim provided, he was well on his way. As his son grew, Wim continued to guide his son, to help him move from understanding to considering his personal responsibility for social change. What is it people need and how can I help create value? He had made the shift from judgment to tolerance, and now from understanding to a desire to make a difference.

As Western Union CEO, Hikmet travels to many of the 200 countries and territories where his company has locations and agents, and when possible, he will bring his son along. Some of those locations are in large, well-established institutions, like the Kroger-owned grocery chain in Colorado where the company is headquartered. Others are small operations, often in far less developed parts of the world.

As a matter of course, Western Union does mystery shopping to see how operations are run and how customers are using Western Union. On his travels, Hikmet will occasionally do some mystery shopping of his own, but true to his style and background in business development, Hikmet can more often be found talking to the local residents, trying to understand their larger financial and banking needs and devising new ways that the company can meet them. By accompanying his father on some of his trips, his son has learned some very valuable lessons. First, he was able to see what his dad does for a living and how he actively engages in the world, whether flying first class to exotic locations and seeing the wonders of the world like the Great Wall of China or venturing into what many would consider extreme hardship environments. In all cases, Hikmet is at ease, which has helped teach his son how to be more open to discovering himself and the world around him.

2. Have a Global Conversation

To empathize, one needs to communicate. And to communicate, one needs to understand the nuances of language and culture. In turn, language and culture can shape one's personality. A person who speaks multiple languages will be exposed and connected to the cultural underpinnings of multiple societies, which can then become a part of their overall (and global) identity.

Many of the global executives interviewed in this book speak multiple languages, and they are equally insistent on speaking multiple languages with their children. For example, Frits van Paasschen only speaks Dutch to his children so they can become fluent in his mother tongue. When they were very young, Maya Strelar-Migotti's children also became fluent in several languages.

What I love about exposing children early to learning languages is that they learn to be comfortable with the uncomfortable. And they become far more understanding when non-native speakers try to learn and express themselves in another language. What's most interesting is when they discover that there is not always a word for that in a different language, or the literal translation can mean something completely different. For example, when my son Tucker and I were having dinner in Mexico, I said "que rico." He asked, somewhat confused, "'How rich,' mommy? That's a weird expression." I explained to him that Spanish phrase is often used when tasting something particularly delicious.

Tucker and I have explored culture through language several times. His first big trip out of the country was with me on business to Zurich and Davos, Switzerland. With support from his teacher, he was excused from classes, but only if he completed some homework assignments: to learn words in the local languages. Switzerland was perfect because he could experience local variations of both German and French. This became a very fun game because many of the signs were written in three different languages, including English, so he could make the translations easily. At first he would laugh when he heard native German speakers put sentences together in English. But then when he saw how sentences are constructed in German, he understood and was able to make a similar connection to how he should try to speak German.

When we went to Mexico, I challenged him to do the same thing. We asked the hotel staff to help by speaking Spanish, not English, with us. We also took several trips off the hotel property to visit local villages, with Tucker again speaking as much of the native language as he could. By the time we boarded the plane back to the states, Tucker was speaking with incredible ease and mastery. But more importantly he was making connections with people from another part of the world. By watching some of the local residents, he made a connection to how people talk and move. He said there was a synchronicity to the sounds and their movements. Those connections only grew, with his appreciation for how colorful the culture is, as reflected in its language, its art, and especially the people.

3. Bring the World Home

Several of the executives talked about the various ways they bring the world home to their children—whether through dinner table conversation about the places they have been, current events discussions, or exploration of arts and culture. Kids learn through the expression of art and music. For example, as they become accustomed to international music and its diversity, they adjust naturally to the various sounds, making the language and genres feel less foreign. Talk to your children, exchange ideas, research online together. And most importantly, make it fun.

Here's something Tucker and I did when he was in second grade, thanks to Barb Knabenbauer, his very open-minded and innovative teacher. That was at a point in my tenure at Cisco when my business travel schedule was quite extensive. Tucker and I decided we needed to bring the places that I traveled home to him and to his classmates. He and I talked with his teacher and came up with the idea of a game called: "Where in the World is Tucker's Mommy?"—much like the children's book series, *Where's Waldo*? At the onset of each trip, I would send clues to the classroom via emails. I would tell the students which oceans I was flying over, the types of food I was eating, the people I was meeting, and the customs I was experiencing. I would share pictures of local landmarks and local art. Sometimes, I would even videotape the experience so the kids could see pictures of how people lived (for example, in India, with cows in the living room, or in classrooms with gravel-covered floors).

As an example, on one of my trips to Beijing I sent the following email:

"I just boarded a plane in San Francisco and I am now traveling over the Pacific Ocean. My flight is very long—about 14 hours. When I land, I will see one of the great wonders of the world: The Great Wall. I will eat exotic foods—like fried pig skin and pigeon—with chopsticks. And I will meet people who many years ago used to be ruled by Emperors. I will see the Forbidden City, the imperial palace from the Ming Dynasty."

Tucker was the only one who knew where I was, so he was able to provide extra hints to the class during the week. When I returned, I would bring local trinkets to the class, and we would talk about the places that I visited and what I had learned. While this isn't the same as traveling themselves, it's a fun and engaging way to bring the world to children and to raise their curiosity about what the world looks like from another child's eyes.

Parents can also help create an environment that fosters looking at everyday things from a more global perspective. It can be as simple as taking a basic homework assignment and putting a global spin on it. For example, children often have to craft stories for their spelling homework. Why not travel the world through the Internet and make that the subject matter, perhaps a story about a place they would like to visit, as opposed to something that is more familiar.

Holidays are another perfect opportunity. I already told you about our blue and silver Hanukkah tree. Hikmet and his wife, who is from India, celebrate Christian, Hindu, and Muslim holidays so that his son experiences the many aspects of his collective heritage.

Computer games can also be a great resource. You have heard my strong opinions about extremely violent video games. But there are many far more appropriate educational games that open up the world to children. Here are some of my favorites:

- **Stack the Countries**—Players are asked questions about a specific country (capital, landmark, major city, continent, and so on) and choose from four multiple-choice answers. Each correct answer unlocks a random country on the child's world map. It is not an easy game, but with trial and error (another important lesson), children can learn and master geography over time. Tucker loves this game because it is so challenging.

- **Wander the World**—A game that lets younger children virtually fly around the world to locations on every continent, with the swish of a finger. They see the flag and several photos of each country. What's nice about this application is that kids also hear music paired with the region of the world that they are visiting.

- **Cafe GeoQuiz**—With a user-friendly interface, children test their knowledge of the planet. The application covers various geography-related material, from capitals and flags to natural extremes, such as the highest points and coldest places.

4. Education on a Global Level

As many of the earlier examples illustrate, there is nothing like being there in person. But I also recognize it is not always possible for many reasons. Here is where our schools can play an important role.

Truly global leaders hold very different expectations for the education processes and environments that their children experience. They insist on global curricula with a sufficient emphasis placed on world dynamics—world history, world politics, world economics, and world cultures—delivered in unique ways (for example, studying World War II as seen through the eyes of the Americans, the British, the Italians, the Germans, and maybe even the Chinese). In a global economy, children cannot afford to grow up ignorant of other countries, cultures, or languages. Unfortunately, research shows that American students are often far less aware of history, politics, and even geography outside the borders of the U.S. Consider some of these statistics from the Global Studies Foundation:

- Large numbers of 18-24 year olds cannot locate significant places on a world map, including the U.S. (11 percent), the Pacific Ocean (29 percent), China (37 percent), Russia (39 percent), and India (56 percent).

- 43 percent are unable to identify Mexico as the largest source of American immigrants today.

- 56 percent are unaware that the European Union is the organization sponsoring the Euro.

- Only 25 percent can identify India and China as countries with one billion people (although 30 percent estimate the U.S. population as 1 to 2 billion) (Harth, 2013).

Historically, many public school curricula have relegated international studies to a segment in a world history class or to international days that are more pageants than they are true learning experiences. But I am beginning to see some very positive changes, albeit still very much the exception than the rule. Once again, here is where parents and global leaders have a responsibility to seek out opportunities for their children, as well as to put pressure on schools—public and private—to consider how they are educating students to be citizens of the world. How we teach our children needs to be reflective of the world today: not disconnected and isolated, but rather highly integrated, interdependent, and connected. Global studies is not a course in and of itself, it should be incorporated into everything that we teach—from the humanities to the social and natural sciences, and even math.

Just consider these examples:

- Most of the students at Sunset Elementary in Miami, Florida, are enrolled in an international magnet program. They learn Spanish, French, or German within the context of a global education. Each grading period focuses on one of four essential aspects of global citizenship: exploring civic responsibilities, gaining cultural awareness, learning about the environment, and understanding the global economy.

- At John Stanford International School (JSIS) for grades K–5 in Seattle, teachers integrate global curricula into conventional units. In language arts, kids read literature from around the world. In science, they study global weather patterns and the effects of erosion in other countries. In math, teachers explain the Japanese way of learning multiplication tables and the Kenyan way of counting numbers.

- Each week at Walter Payton College Preparatory High School in Chicago, students choose two 80-minute world-learning seminars from about 60 choices. Sam Dyson, a physics teacher, offers a seminar in Zulu language and culture. With new languages come new concepts.

- Students at Walter Payton also choose a second language: Chinese, Japanese, Latin, Spanish, or French. For the next school year, Arabic may be added. A sister school and an exchange program for every language help students deepen their learning.

Homa Sabet Tavangar makes these points with great eloquence in her book, *Growing Up Global: Raising Children to Be At Home in the World*: "A successful integration of international topics in the school day increases empathy and connection with diverse people; it also helps to hone critical thinking skills and make the study of topics like science, math, and foreign language apply to very real issues confronting the world. If this integration does occur, then a program like an International Day will feel more like a culmination of the learning that has been taking place, not a stage show. It would also reinforce your efforts at home" (2009).

As I said, there are examples of programs that support exactly what Homa and many of the global leaders espouse. I have listed some below, but please be aware, these are just a sampling and only from America, which is not to infer that there are not many more, in the U.S. and in countries around the world, that are worth noting and promoting.

Global Nomads Group (www.gng.org) connects North American classrooms with places like Afghanistan and Antarctica, using interactive media and technology so young people can learn about and discuss global issues affecting their lives.

The **Global Kidz Lab** in Denver offers a kindergarten through middle school immersion program. Students learn Spanish, French, and Chinese language and culture in small classroom settings. Using a technology-enabled collaborative learning methodology, students travel the world virtually to learn language in the context of the cultures where those languages are spoken. Similar programs are offered in many cities across the United States.

On the east coast, the **Middlebury-Monterey Language Academies** offers a summer language immersion camp for middle school students, with a focus on Spanish, French, German, Chinese, and Arabic culture.

Governments and corporations are also supporting a more global curriculum. With support from the government of China and corporations including Motorola, Chicago Public Schools co-initiated the Confucius Institute (Confuciusinstitutechicago. org). Housed at a public high school, it provides learning resources to help substantially increase the number of students learning Chinese. Chicago now has the largest Chinese language program in the United States.

Teachers and parents looking for resources for the home or classroom may also want to visit **globalbooksforkids.com**, which offers a comprehensive list of reviews for the latest children's books—in the realm of multiculturalism and global education topics. The site features books from the Middle East to East India and from Asia to Latin America, along with suggestions for global immersion. Scholastic.com also highlights a number of exceptional programs on its website.

Before I close this section, I want to introduce you to the Think Global School (http://thinkglobalschool.org), a nonprofit organization that offers high school students the opportunity to complete a high school curriculum while visiting up to 12 countries. The curriculum at Think Global School maintains a strong focus on the core subjects of science, mathematics, and literature, while providing outside the classroom experiences that teach lifelong lessons in critical thinking, social justice, and global citizenry. Founder Joann McPike started the organization after looking for a program that would teach her son different ways of seeing the world: "We looked at schools in America, Canada, Australia, and Europe. The problem with any high school is that you are taught a certain way of thinking, a certain history, and a certain way of seeing the world. It's all very localized, very nationalized...Yes, there are other schools with an English language curriculum and an international student body. Yes, there are traveling classes, and school trips, and year abroad programs, but to actually take these children and their teachers to 12 different countries when they're in high school is a very different vision."

Interestingly, my friend and colleague Marthin DeBeer, former chief innovation officer for Cisco, says his daughter did something very similar in college. She just returned from a semester-at-sea program, on a ship that was rigged out as a university. The 400 students on board visited 20 countries from the Mediterranean to South America over a four-month period. He says the program broadened her perspective. As a film student, she realized it's not about making one film for everyone, but many pictures to meet many different needs.

This has always been an important issue for Marthin, who was raised in South Africa. Growing up in what he described as a highly prejudiced society, and now living in San Jose, California and travelling the world for work, he wanted his children to have the same broad perspective. He has raised his children to be very curious, to want to travel extensively—something his wife is not always happy about—but he is confident they are prepared (as a well-known citizen of the universe would say) to live well and prosper.

Global leaders think big and think forward. Those who are parents have the unique privilege and pleasure to explore the future, from the dinner table or the market square, hand in hand with their children. It's not always easy, but it can be tremendous fun. And it is, without a doubt, the most important work of all.

SECTION 4
Essential Leadership in Action

SECTION IV
Essential Leadership in Action

In section II of the book, I shared the 10 essential traits that I have found to characterize those executives who thrive in a rapidly changing, highly unpredictable, and interconnected and interdependent world. Along the way, I have introduced you to many of those executives. Now, I have the opportunity to give you a closer look at seven of these individuals and how the essential traits contribute to their exceptional leadership capabilities.

As you have learned, leadership happens in context, not from the pages of textbooks. As such, the profiles that follow illustrate how these individuals are applying many of the essential traits in the context of their current positions. I believe that each of these leaders possesses most if not all of the essential traits, but as you read their stories, you will see certain leaders exhibiting more of a certain trait (or combination of traits) compared to others. That is simply a function of the context in which they are leading within the confines of the profiles. I wish you could know these individuals like I know them and like those who have had the opportunity to work alongside them. I could write a book about each one of them individually.

That said, I believe the profiles will give you a good picture of the essential traits in action. Consider as you read their stories:

- how Wim Elfrink of Cisco turned empathy into a business case in the service of market innovation
- how Jim Whitehurst's authenticity has served him well leading both a traditional and a very nontraditional business environment
- how Maya Strelar-Migotti balances control and chaos to support large-scale productivity and innovation on the edge simultaneously within a 6,000 person worldwide and highly competitive organization
- how Hikmet Ersek has the courage to recreate a 162 year-old business model while embarking upon making things less ambiguous for business and human good
- how Hannah Kain has turned collaboration into a competitive advantage in supply-chain management
- how a strong sense of self enabled Sanjeev Bikhchandani to go against what society expected to become one of India's most successful entrepreneurs
- how sense of self guides Fritz van Paasschen as he leads an organization that operates in almost every corner of the world.

These are just some of the examples of the essential traits in action that you will find as you read further. I encourage you to go explore and find your own.

"THINK WITH ME, DREAM WITH ME"

Wim Elfrink

Executive Vice President, Industry Solutions & Chief
Globalisation Officer, Cisco

Beyond brilliant, there is an entertaining air of the mad professor about Wim Elfrink, executive vice president, Industry Solutions, and chief globalisation officer, Cisco Systems, Inc. When he speaks, I know that his brain cells are firing far faster than his mouth can articulate his thoughts. Rather than the standard corporate attire of heavily starched white shirts and pressed suits, Wim usually shows up in an unpressed button-down shirt, sleeves rolled up, his grey hair in need of a trim and appearing almost electrified by what's going on in that brain of his. A master chess player and 42-time marathoner, Wim will draw you in with his warmth and sincerity, but his insights about all matters related to the complex, global landscape are what command your attention.

Born on a small island in the Netherlands, Wim is what I call a corporate global nomad. He has lived all over the world, held management positions with big brand global companies (including Digital Equipment, Xerox, and HP), is fluent in several languages, and adapts fluidly to whatever culture he is operating within, except perhaps (as he would readily admit) the corporate culture.

In 2006, Cisco CEO John Chambers tapped Wim to make Cisco a truly global company. At the time, Wim was successfully running Cisco's $8 billion services business. One of the most impressive CEOs with whom I have had the pleasure to work, John was known for anticipating and capitalizing on emerging trends, which had been well rewarded by the financial markets, and had built Cisco into a $40 billion technology company. The next big market move for John was globalisation, on a much larger scale than previously undertaken. Rather than just trying to lower production costs or find new markets for existing products, John sought to develop new products and new talent to meet the needs of a changing world. John was ready to invest more than a billion dollars in the initiative, but he needed a bold thinker to achieve his vision. He called on Wim to build Cisco's Globalisation Centre East (GCE) in Bangalore, India.

Sleepless in Bangalore

What would become Cisco's second world headquarters, with more than 10,000 employees, was essentially a barren field when Wim arrived in 2006. His first step was to relocate his family from their comfortable home in Los Altos, California to a new house in India. He handpicked a team of adventurous souls to follow him, many of whom he calls pathfinders for their willingness to seek a new course for the company. Still, it was not easy. Relocation to Bangalore was considered to be a hardship assignment.

While the team embraced the experience, they were reminded by Wim to be "frustration proof," a mindset that guided the executives as they helped build the company's second headquarters and define its globalisation strategy. While a stark contrast to what these executives were used to, Wim felt that full immersion in the culture would be critical to his team's mission. It would prove later to be equally critical to the broader globalisation mission for the company as well.

"Think With Me"

On one of my earliest trips to Bangalore, I had the opportunity to attend a meeting Wim was holding with his team. He began with an invitation: "Think with me. Dream with me," immediately engaging his audience in a provocative dialogue about a marketplace characterized by hyper-growth and unmet needs. Wim challenged his team to think differently, to suspend their judgment about how things are and consider instead what it would be like "if…" He believes thinking differently is funda-mental to conceiving new products and more importantly for creating new industries. Wim foretold of a massive shift whereby the combined economic output of the world's emerging markets would start to surpass that of the world's developed and advanced economies. To succeed in this new world order, he said Cisco would need to respond to changing market needs more quickly, especially in light of new competitors emerging from unexpected places, producing unanticipated products, and creating significant market shocks. That, he said, would require the company to be more strategic in how it develops business models, partnerships, ecosystems, and solutions to address new kinds of markets and customers worldwide. On a more personal note, he explained why he came to India as a corporate entrepreneur to help transform Cisco from a multinational corporation to a global innovator. He said he and his team needed to think out of the box, and to do so, they would need to be out of the box themselves.

Wim called on Cisco's senior leadership and his new organization to commit to achieving three primary objectives:

- to develop Cisco's second global headquarters (Globalisation Centre East) that would help transform Cisco into a truly global company

- to position the company for growth in emerging markets through strategically placed innovation centers that could focus on creating new products and solutions to meet local market needs

- to recruit and leverage talent from a much larger marketplace, essentially the world.

To think with Wim is both intellectually stimulating and emotionally exhausting. He continually pushes those around him to anticipate changes that are coming. Wim sees what is possible, especially with the accelerated rate of new technology development, and carefully considers the impacts on the market from geopolitical, economic, and social perspectives. He wonders, just because something is possible, is the market ready to handle it? Wim and his leadership team talk about what the world will look like in 30 to 50 years. That's quite a lot for a company to think about, especially when most businesses consider long-term planning to be a three- to five-year exercise at most. But for

Wim, with the pace of change accelerated by technology, these changes are just around the corner and the time is now for the company to make strategic decisions to get ready for what's ahead. Wim is a dreamer of the highest order, but he is also a realist and recognizes that some people can get overwhelmed thinking about the future to the point where they may deny that the changes could or will happen. I liken this to the Jetson's dynamic. It was entertaining to watch how, in the old cartoons, technology changed the lives of George and Jane Jetson. After all, who would ever believe that we would microwave our food, that robots would vacuum our floors, and that people would commute to work by plane?

Wim leads in the context of a world that is changing rapidly and dramatically. To sustain market relevance and prominence, Wim believes Cisco, and especially the globalisation team, needs to produce commercial, environmental, and societal value. To do so, Wim says you need to understand what is happening in the world:

There is already a shortage of food, water, power, housing, and education to meet the needs of the 7 billion people that currently inhabit the globe.

The world's middle class—defined as people with annual incomes ranging from $6,000 to $30,000—is growing by 70 million people a year. These consumers need communications, transportation, and housing to assume their place in the world economy.

Globally, population is shifting from rural to urban areas, with an average of 180,000 persons per day expected to move from the countryside to big cities over the next decade.

Three billion people will be connected to the Internet over the next 10 years, many of them before they have access to electricity or running water.

Make Needs the Business

Wim set out to build an enduring organization in India, not just generate financial returns. For Wim, it's not either-or; it's both. He believes the value that a company creates should be measured not simply in terms of short-term profits, but rather in how it creates the conditions necessary to sustain its long-term viability. And that means understanding and making the needs of people core to the business purpose, as opposed to a requirement. To do so, Wim and his team identified that they would need to develop technology to help connect communities (to support massive urbanization), and improve the delivery of healthcare and education (to support a rising middle class); both would generate greater value for society. In his words, "We have a responsibility to society. The greed has to be over! We need to make needs the business."

Innovation
Making needs the business is also fundamental to innovation in Wim's world and that, he says, requires empathy. By more deeply understanding the experiences of others, you are in a better position to come up with products and services that meet their needs, and in the process, maybe even change the world.

Historically, Wim says, the most important innovations have fundamentally changed society. The chimney changed how and with whom people spent their days and more importantly their nights; the printing press revolutionized how we share information (as the Internet is doing today); air-conditioning populated regions previously considered uninhabitable; and social media is changing how people communicate and collaborate in real time. Wim's mission is to create a set of technological solutions that will spawn new industries and have a similarly dramatic impact on society.

Wim also appreciates the need to experiment and to master the art of failure. He openly admits that there were plenty of failures as Cisco strived to develop and launch customer solutions for emerging markets, but like anything, you get better with practice. As a result, the team developed processes that make it possible for the company to fail cheaper and faster. And with a better aptitude for experimentation, Cisco can bring more innovation to market.

One of Wim's biggest challenges was integrating this more global perspective into the corporate culture and priorities. About three years into the assignment, Wim realized that the strategy he (and John) had developed to ensure Cisco's continued relevancy in an emerging global marketplace might not be fully understood by Cisco's leadership. In India, his team could see the opportunity firsthand—to them, it was crystal clear—but they had not been able to generate that kind of interest and support back at headquarters. Wim realized his most important responsibility was no longer building and executing Cisco's globalisation strategy, but rather bringing other executives on board, literally. He needed to get them to see the potential for themselves to understand why Cisco not only wanted to, but had to, do business in his part of the world. But most were not overly excited at the prospects of flying to India and immersing themselves in the place and the culture.

During one of my (at this point many) visits to India, I had coffee with Wim soon after he had returned from an operating committee meeting at the corporate offices in San Jose. He expressed his frustration with the resistance he was receiving from his executive peers and some of the senior vice presidents critical to the globalisation effort. Although John was no less convinced that globalisation was critical to Cisco's success, he had to shift his focus to help lead the company through the massive macroeconomic meltdown of 2008-2009.

We were sitting on the couch in his Bangalore office, a room resembling a fishbowl with four glass walls in the middle of the workspace—a testament to Wim's belief in openness and transparency. Wim, who is very action-oriented, had hoped the senior executives would recognize the urgency of the company to globalise and move faster in enabling the needed changes in business models, management systems, and organizational changes. As Wim describes it, globalisation and the cultural change that is needed is a 10-year journey. Cisco may not have reached its destination yet, but focusing on globalisation as a priority has enabled the company to change course to the right direction.

It is not uncommon for such revolutionary changes to be resisted by those who are comfortable with the status quo or who do not or cannot see the value. And it is not uncommon for such large-scale efforts to be sabotaged by those who fear the unknown.

Over several conversations during this trip, the team came up with a solution: To leverage Cisco's signature executive development program, the Executive Action Learning Forum (E-ALF), to bring resources to Wim's globalisation mission. (You can read more about E-ALF in the practices section in chapter 6.)

As a result, Cisco flew nearly 65 high-potential leaders into Bangalore and Beijing. There, they were assigned to highly innovative, strategic projects critical to work being done by Wim, as well as by Cisco's president of Asia and its chief innovation officer. The 65 participants were divided into sub-teams that mimicked the larger organization, with representatives from engineering, finance, human resources, supply chain, operations, sales, and marketing. Each team was also comprised of individuals from different theaters (or regions) around the globe. Over a 16-week period, these high-potential leaders immersed themselves in the market because only then could they fully understand what the people needed and the corresponding opportunities for Cisco.

The teams were charged with identifying and developing business opportunities within emerging economies from the ground up, and they were hugely successful in doing so. Because they saw firsthand what was happening in these markets, they naturally became evangelists for the strategic opportunities Cisco had to create to deliver value, both by operating within and serving these markets. Most importantly, in order for these leaders to be successful on their specific projects, they had to breathe new life into the globalisation opportunity by building support among the key decision makers at Cisco. The E-ALF participants initiated and nurtured a strategic dialogue about the commercial and societal value of their initiatives to convince the senior executives to prioritize their projects. The multiplier effect was impressive. By the time they were done, these 65 people had convinced nearly 1000 of the most senior decision makers to seriously consider the market opportunities, as well as the organizational challenges, inherent in globalisation.

One of the most important innovations to come out of the work of teams at the Globalisation Centre East is the Smart+Connected

Communities initiative. In 2009 Cisco unveiled the blueprint for a network that wirelessly connects the physical aspects of a community: real estate, utilities, transportation, safety, education, healthcare, government, and even entertainment. Cisco is embedding networking technology in urban design for economic, social, and environmental sustainability.

The technology is already at work in existing cities, as well as in those under development. In South Korea, Cisco is partnering with an American developer and a Korean construction firm to build a new 1,500-acre city called New Songdo on reclaimed land. Cisco is providing the technological "plumbing" that connects and runs the city, which is being built to the highest sustainability standards. Construction is expected to be complete by 2016. By 2012, it was already a thriving city with 20,000 residents. Songdo will be a template for new cities built from scratch across the globe.

Creating Collaborative Partnerships

Wim believes in the power of collaborative private-public partnerships. He says globalisation increases the need for enduring local relationships with government officials, with nongovernmental organizations (NGOs), with suppliers, and with both business partners and competitors. Partnerships are critical to help global leaders ensure that agendas are aligned when possible, especially as economic, geopolitical, and social circumstances change—and they can change frequently in emerging markets. Certainly, agendas will not always be 100 percent in sync, but even competitors can often find some commonality or shared purpose, such as ensuring a healthy economy so that consumers can afford to buy their respective products or services. With others, the common denominator is focused on solving broader societal needs, such as improving healthcare, education, or the environment, often through a combination of public policy and technological enhancements. For Wim, having a societal purpose extends beyond his professional life. He and his wife Kate lead by example with their personal commitment of time and money to early childhood education. You have to do more than *do* business in a country—you have to *earn* business, according to Wim. "It's no longer good enough just to serve your shareholders only. You must serve the communities and partner with the governments with which you do, or want to do, business."

Wim believes that corporate leaders need to take more responsibility for how businesses work with government, as opposed to just trying to influence, fight, or live with regulation. In his view, business has become far too complicated for individual governments to understand and regulate. By carefully considering the geopolitical, economic, social, and ecological factors at play in a more holistic manner, corporate leaders can help educate government, and even gain more flexibility and trust through self-regulation. He asks, "How do leaders take the socially responsible high road when faced with market and investor pressures? How do they make this core to global leadership, versus something that's nice to have if and when circumstances allow?"

Under Wim's leadership, in 2008 Cisco committed to investing $20 million to develop the Guanghua Cisco Leadership Institute at Peking University in China. The goal is to develop homegrown Chinese research and executive development programs based on a curriculum of collaboration, innovation, and globalisation. According to Wim, caring for the community (and the people) where a company does business is not just altruistic. It is good business and critical to the success of any globalisation effort.

The Corporate Brain

Wim believes that formal organizational structures can be too rigid to accommodate the multidirectional pathways necessary to support constructive collaboration and the needs of global markets. Instead, he encourages self-organizing efforts (remember the theory of living systems) that bring networks of passionate and invested employees, partners, and customers together to work toward common goals and objectives. When people are uniquely invested in the outcome of such work, they show up with greater levels of accountability and engagement, providing what is, in a sense, a collective corporate brain that can be leveraged for the purposes of globalisation.

Successful globalisation efforts require leadership to be deliberate in where and how they access, deploy, and develop talent and capabilities for the organization. He says "It is no longer about reading about or educating leaders on globalisation anymore…you have to have the guts as an executive to live where globalisation is happening." He references how a progressive company like Schneider Electric moved its executive team to Hong Kong in order for them to more fully become immersed in the Chinese market.

Good leadership, according to Wim, is more about asking the right questions than having all the right answers. Asking "what if" is more relevant than proposing what worked in the past. As leaders get older, Wim comments that they can become prisoners of their own experiences. He believes this is the kiss of death for a global leader.

Wim is redefining what it means to be a global business leader. When I pressed him to help me understand what he thinks it takes to be a truly effective global leader, the portrait he painted was one of a complex person who can hold multiple, simultaneous tensions. In his words, "The true global leader must be intelligent, curious, always questioning; empathetic yet still able to make judgments; humble yet ever so bold; nomadic yet always rooted; and most importantly the global leader must know what he does not know." Wim also believes that to be truly global one must be multilingual. Most of the leaders featured in this book agree with him on this. Wim adds that it's not so much about the ability to speak other languages, as it is the process of learning the language that immerses one into the nuances and texture of a culture.

Wim also notes that global leaders must operate with strong ethics and transparency. Ethics that were once associated with altruism, he now associates with capitalism. In his words: "There are so many more stakeholders to consider that you must understand the needs of many." A deep understanding of global needs, he says, translates into successful business outcomes.

OPENING UP LEADERSHIP AND ORGANIZATIONAL POTENTIAL

Jim Whitehurst
CEO, Red Hat

What's a nice southern boy, known best for turning around Delta Air Lines—one of the oldest companies in a highly regulated industry—doing running Red Hat, a pioneer in open source technology with a business model that even the leaders of some of the most cutting edge technology companies have a hard time fully appreciating? Just spend some time with Red Hat CEO Jim Whitehurst and it will become clear. Jim thinks big and boldly about the future of management and organizational structure, but without losing sight of the fundamental principles behind what it takes to engage and lead others.

Jim has a way—perhaps it is his southern upbringing—that makes you feel as comfortable as if you are talking to your brother or the boy next door, while at the same time intriguing you with his unique combination of scholarly insight and just plain common sense. While he readily admits he does not have all the answers, he spends a lot of time questioning how business models, and in turn the role of the leader, need to change to optimize the potential of the knowledge worker in a truly global information economy.

Jim graduated from Rice University with a bachelor's degree in computer science and a dream to work in Silicon Valley. Preferring the business side of technology, and also armed with an economics degree, Jim joined the Boston Consulting Group (BCG). "I loved every aspect of consulting, especially the problem solving," says Jim, which led him back to BCG, after getting his MBA from Harvard.

As a partner in the firm's newly opened Atlanta office, Jim began doing a lot of hard-core financial work for Delta Air Lines. That's why, within hours after the terrorist attack on September 11, 2001, Delta's

CEO tapped Jim to be the company treasurer. With all of its planes grounded, Delta was in jeopardy of not making payroll at the end of the month. What the company needed and what they got with Jim was a creative finance guy who could make the deals necessary to keep the airline in business.

But Delta's problems had been building for years (Jim says as the result of losing customer focus) and the company plunged into bankruptcy in 2005. Once again, Delta tapped Jim, this time as COO. Over the next two years, he focused on turning the company around. And it worked. Delta went from dead last for on-time performance to number one among the major carriers in just six months. By the time Delta emerged from bankruptcy, J.D. Powers had ranked the airline number two in customer satisfaction in its class.

How did he do it? By listening, and responding, to employees. Too often he says, companies ask their employees for ideas—the proverbial suggestion box—but rarely do they answer back. Maybe it's because they decide not to move forward with those suggestions, but Jim says a thoughtful response, even if it is no, is well received by employees. Asking for ideas and not responding, he says, is worse than not asking at all.

Although none of this is particularly new, what's different about Jim is that he leads by example. He invites employees to email him personally and fulfills his promise by answering them. He proudly tells a tale about receiving an email from some mechanics about a sensitive corporate decision. The email invited Jim to join them for a barbecue lunch, so he picked up the phone and called the guys. They were astonished and impressed, confessing that they had a bet going among themselves, as to whether it was Jim who actually read and responded to the emails or if he delegated the responsibility to some subordinate.

At Delta—and now at Red Hat—everyone has Jim's email address, and they use it. At Delta, Jim says there were times he would receive a thousand emails a day; he even bought a special attachment for his exercise bike so he could go through them during his morning workout.

For executives who say they don't have time, Jim says they don't have a choice. As he explains it, we are raising a generation that expects to be listened to. We have given them the tools to communicate. Now, we need to give them an answer.

Whether it was with answering emails or while throwing bags with the ground crew on Christmas, Jim got his employees' attention. They understood and did what he asked them to do. It was hard work, but it turned the airline around.

When it came time for Jim to leave Delta, a decision he made after the post-bankruptcy board brought in one of their own to be CEO, he considered his options, and there were many given his success. While Jim says he is not a self-reflective person (I believe differently), he does have a keen understanding of who he is as a person, another essential leadership quality. It's not just about knowing his strengths and weaknesses, but it's also about knowing what he wants to do and what he values. For example, Jim had a lot of lucrative offers from private equity companies that wanted him to continue to be a turnaround guy. He says, ironically, that one of the reasons he was good at implementing the hard decisions, such as layoffs, was that people knew it was painful for him and they respected him for it. But in the long run, it was not his calling.

That kind of authenticity is another of Jim's strong suits, and one that he says is an absolute necessity in today's more socially connected and socially aware world. Gone are the days when a CEO could adopt an external persona of how he thinks a leader should behave. Today, Jim says, people can smell a fake, and even if they can't, someone will catch you out of character and share it with the rest of the world, via Twitter or Facebook or YouTube…or the next generation of social media. So, he says, you need to ask yourself, who are you, really?

"Authenticity" is a word they use a lot at Red Hat. Authenticity creates trust, and trust is fundamental to a more collaborative approach to software development, says Jim. But he admits he did not create the culture of trust and collaboration. He self-selected into it and now continues to nurture it as CEO. When he got the call about Red Hat, he knew it was a fit. It got him back to his technology roots, but it was also a company applying a fundamentally different business model to technology. Jim knew he could do something big at Red Hat. At a more established company with a traditional business model, Jim was confident he could have a positive impact, but he wanted to radically change how business is done—not just for the sake of change, but for the sake of doing it better.

Finding a better way to make software is the underlying driver behind the open source movement. Rather than restricting access by requiring paid licenses to use its software, Red Hat believes sharing the code for its Linux product with a larger community of developers ultimately creates more value. The only rule: If you take the code and do something with it, you have to share the fruits of your labor under the same terms.

This model also requires a strong belief system: a belief that it not only creates a better product, but that it is compatible with making a profit. As Jim put it, "We have to believe that better results come when broader communities work together, whether that's competitors, business partners, people we don't even know. It's in our DNA."

Getting people to believe what you believe is nirvana for the global leader, according to Jim. The first step is getting people to do what you want them to do, but through engagement rather than control. The next level is getting them to think the way you want them to think—not necessarily what you think, but how you want them to think: creatively, collaboratively. And finally comes belief.

As a leader, Jim believes his job is to get people to believe in the mission of the company. Once you have instilled that belief, he says, people approach problem-solving thinking differently. Rather than just figuring out how to get around the wall, they are willing, if they could, to walk through the wall for you. They have a passion that only comes from understanding the broader meaning behind why they are doing what they do.

He also credits his success with having the right leadership team in place: peers that he trusts. For him, there is no secret formula to selecting his team members. They simply have to have the right intellectual and emotional quotient. Are they good at their jobs? Do they work hard? Are they excited about what they do? Can they thrive in a less structured, somewhat disorganized environment? Jim recognizes there are a lot of very brilliant people working for other highly successful technology companies who would not fit at Red Hat. It's not a value judgment on his part; it's about fit.

Jim is always searching for new ways of thinking about how to best structure and lead organizations in this new, more collaborative business environment. How do you find the right balance between setting direction and letting teams self-organize around their work? How do you balance the need for creativity and innovation with the demands of Wall Street? How do you work with competitors who do not share your belief structure? Jim says there are some academics beginning to publish work around "Collaboration Management 2.0," but there is still relatively little known or published on the topic. He continually asks his head of HR to seek out new research or individuals writing about the topic; he talks to other executives about how they are dealing with similar issues; and he engages his employees. Mostly, he admits, he is figuring it out as he goes along. And for this highly adaptable and exceptionally authentic executive, that's okay. After all, it's all about being open.

DREAMING ON THE EDGE

Hannah Kain

CEO, ALOM

Hannah Kain has always been a dreamer, whether as the young girl in Denmark who imagined herself as a race car driver or today as the CEO of a highly successful supply-chain company serving some of the world's leading corporations. In fact, when I met Hannah, one of the first things she told me was "My word for the year is 'dream.'" (She chooses a new one each year.) Dreaming is also an essential part of Hannah's approach to leadership and innovation. It has helped her see through the tough times and fuels the ingenuity and willingness to take risks that has made it possible for her company to expand dramatically in recent years. As she put it: "If you think about it, everything is made up: the iPhone, the automobile, even the United States."

The first thing you see when you meet Hannah is her engaging smile, which draws you in and invites you to consider the possibilities. She doesn't just consider; she does, with a fun-loving, yet scrappy (get it done) kind of style all her own. She proudly tells the story about her first business venture at the age of four, when she and her brother dug up some primroses and started selling them door-to-door. It was the perfect business model, says Hannah. No cost of goods, no overhead. Perfect, that is, until her father found out, which, Hannah laughs, is why she has always hated regulation. She says it limits flexibility and adaptability, critical components for innovation and two of the qualities she likes the most about Americans.

On the other hand, Hannah says Americans fall short compared to other cultures when it comes to collaboration. "Americans tend to excel as individuals, while the Danish are more collaborative," explains Hannah. And she questions whether Japan would be more competitive today if its culture were not as insular. Growing up in Denmark, Hannah was taught the value of teamwork early in life. There, she says, schools intentionally pair the weak with the strong and grade the students on the success of the team, not their individual performance. That lesson has served her well in both business and politics.

Since her floral adventure, Hannah has undertaken many things at a surprisingly young age. As a preteen, she ran the back office for her father, much to the chagrin of her father's accountant when he found out he had been corresponding on business matters with a 12 year-old girl. At 17, Hannah got a taste of politics, first organizing and running a student organization in high school and later at the university level. While still in her teens, she was already a frequent public speaker, the co-host of her own weekly radio show, and a columnist for the largest newspaper in Denmark. Then at age 21, she became the youngest person ever to run for the Danish parliament. Along the way, Hannah met some very influential people, including the foreign and energy ministers, and a colleague who eventually became a European commissioner. Those connections propelled her to the world stage, where she worked as a part of the Danish Parliament's delegation to the United Nations.

Hannah understands the power of connections, as well as collaborative networks. Her company, ALOM, has just 100 employees, plus 150 or so contract workers. But if you count her business partners around the world, Hannah has a network that is more than 3000 strong. Building a reliable and resourceful network has been essential to her company's ability to scale quickly to meet growing customer demands. ALOM provides clients with supply-chain services ranging from order management, online shopping carts, and customer support, all the way through fulfillment, reverse logistics, and advanced digital media and print solutions. Supply chain has always required collaboration, given the need to connect a wide range of players from manufacturer to market. But Hannah sees even greater opportunities in an increasingly complex global environment. Borders—literally and figuratively—are far less defined, and as she puts it "Things are more complex while time is being squeezed. Our skill set is facilitating how it all fits together."

The quality of ALOM's global networks has given her Fortune 100 clients the confidence to outsource their mission critical supply-chain functions to Hannah's company, freeing them up to focus on what they do best. Because Hannah's clients depend on global supply chains, Hannah has to have a global presence. Less than a decade ago, when some of her customers expressed a need for her to handle more of their international business, Hannah began looking at how she could most effectively and expediently expand to meet their requirements. By collaborating with business partners around the world—including some who are also her competitors—she has managed to quickly establish an international presence, shipping out of 16 locations and managing dozens of new global programs. She leverages both the infrastructure and workforces of her business partners, as opposed to trying to build it herself. Financially it works, too, with revenues having increased by 60 percent in recent years.

Hannah admits that she is not intimidated by many things, a quality she attributes to her father who, as a concentration camp survivor, often spoke about things he wished he could have done at an earlier age. That instilled in Hannah a drive to live life without regrets, which sometimes requires risk taking.

Hannah says companies that are more hierarchical in nature tend to be more cautious and less willing to take risks. That, she says, inhibits creativity. Given the importance of the ecosystem not only to her business but also to an expanding international marketplace, Hannah believes global leaders should take heed: "I am willing to take the risk because the pluses are enormous. If you don't trust people, you create a culture where two signatures are always required," and she says that takes too much time. Hannah explains the increasing importance of speed this way: "I am in the process-innovation business. It used to be that a customer would order a product and it would show up in four to six weeks, no problem. Now, four to six weeks is the time it takes someone to invent an entirely new product."

Hannah's upbringing also developed her desire to be straight-forward with people—an attribute that is highly valued in Denmark. As CEO, her mission is to run a company that treats everyone fairly and with which people want to do business. "That's the Danish management style in me," Hannah proudly states. Like many of the global leaders interviewed for this book, Hannah is keenly aware of her role as CEO and the fact that her perspectives have been shaped by the social norms of the society in which she was raised. For that reason, she surrounds herself with individuals who can provide her with different points of view and help her be thoughtful about cultural differences as she moves around the globe. Having a diverse team helps her stay true to herself, while being sensitive to the needs of the larger world in which she and her business function.

Hannah spends much of her time travelling around the world, meeting with existing business partners and evaluating new relationships. To make sure it's the right cultural fit, Hannah says, "I need to jive with the top executives. We spend a lot of time talking about the industry and exchanging ideas on how to solve various problems. I learn something new and important every time I meet with my partners and my competitors."

Whether hiring a new employee or forming a business partnership, Hannah seeks out people who are resourceful: "It's no longer about finding someone who can do a particular job in a specific environment. I need someone who can figure out what's needed and then how to get it done." Instead of asking how good they are at making this or doing that, she asks herself: How resourceful are they? How big is their network? How trustworthy are they? Can they collaborate? The way Hannah sees it, having a network with resources is critical if you want to do something you have never tried before or want to expand in markets and cultures where you have never worked.

Hannah meets with every new employee in order to personally share where the company is going. She provides them with a one-page business plan that highlights the key things the business needs to accomplish and the values that the organization lives by. Most importantly, she talks to each employee about how that person fits into the overall plan. And she listens. In doing so, Hannah creates two-way communication from the start, out to the organization and back to her as the leader.

Leaders, she says, need to be out and about—in their companies, in their expanded networks, and in the world, listening and looking for new ideas. She admits it's not easy: "Listening for ideas takes a special skill—to let go of how you think things need to be and open your mind to how things could be." She references Steve Jobs as a global leader who was willing to follow his instincts for ideas. But it all comes back to risk; a behavior that she recognizes is frowned upon in many organizations.

The result is a culture where people are afraid to take chances for fear of being fired.

Her answer is to reward risk—something she also admits is easier in a smaller company. She is always willing to listen to ideas, even the bad ones, and she rewards people for sharing. She recalls an acquisition when the people in the combined company were not aligned. "I needed to make a lot of symbolic gestures, to find the teachable moments and recognize people when they were demonstrating the kind of collaborative behaviors we need."

Hannah believes in investing in the success of others. After she and her husband emigrated from Denmark, Hannah went from being a well-known and distinguished businesswoman and political leader to working as a marketing director in a small company in the U.S. She has come a long way since then and is grateful to be in the position today where she has so many opportunities. As a successful CEO with a long list of awards and distinctions to her name, Hannah sees it as her ultimate responsibility to create those same opportunities for others. As she learned as a child, she is judged not by her own performance, but by that of the entire team, which includes both her employees and her broader network. Globalisation, to Hannah, is all about collaboration and creating an ecosystem of partners aligned to create value and shared prosperity in the markets in which they do business.

A BETTER IDEA

Sanjeev Bikhchandani
Founder, Info Edge (Naukri.com)

As the son of a doctor working for the Indian government, Sanjeev Bikhchandani had a fairly common childhood. He lived in modest government housing, played with the children of other government officers, and was expected to pursue a career in medicine or engineering. But Sanjeev had other ideas. From the time he was in 7th or 8th grade, he knew he wanted to be an entrepreneur. "I knew early that I wanted to be doing my own thing, setting my own priorities and, most importantly, creating something different," he said. "But to do so, I knew that I would have to challenge what I was raised to become." And he did, becoming one of the most successful Internet entrepreneurs in India.

Sanjeev has always had high aspirations. He laughed as he recalled a conversation he had as a young boy of six with one of his father's patients, the chief justice on the Indian Supreme Court who was serving as the country's president for a month. When the acting president of India asked Sanjeev if he would ever want to be president, Sanjeev did not hesitate to answer, "Yes, but not for a month, for five years."

As a high-performing student, Sanjeev was accepted into the prestigious and highly competitive Indian Institutes of Technology (IIT), where only one out of every 50 applicants is accepted. But he turned down the opportunity, choosing instead to enroll in St. Stephen College at Delhi University where he earned a bachelor's degree in economics, followed by a postgraduate diploma in management from the Indian Institute of Management in Ahmedabad. Deciding not to go to IIT was highly unusual for a man of Sanjeev's upbringing, as most of his peers were conditioned to aspire to attend what Sanjeev refers to as the "IIT factory" and be content with the steady job and secure income it would help ensure. Sanjeev took another path, but he never lost sight of the strong values his parents had taught him: the importance of education, hard work, decency, courtesy, honesty, respect for others, and putting the community's interests ahead of his own.

While living at his parent's home and teaching at a couple of business schools on the weekend, Sanjeev started his first company, Info Edge, in 1990. But the income from his side jobs and the revenues from his company's first product—a salary survey report—were not enough to make ends meet. Sanjeev had to get help from his first angel investor, his wife Surabhi, who worked as a manager with Nestle. That experience taught Sanjeev a valuable lesson: "If you want to keep the dream afloat, you don't care what the neighbors and relatives say about who wears the pants in your house."

But it was his empathy for the circumstances of others and his powers of observation that led him to the one big idea that made his fortune and is helping change the fortunes of those around him.

It came in 1996, shortly after Sanjeev attended a conference where he was introduced to the still relatively new business potential of the Internet. At approximately the same time, he observed that many of his fellow Indians read business magazines backward, starting first with the want ads. Putting the two together, Sanjeev had the idea for naukri.com, which has become India's top job search and employment website. It's important to note that when Sanjeev first had the idea for naukri.com, the website that would become Monster.com had only been live for two or three years and was anything but well known outside the United States.

Enthused by the possibilities, Sanjeev called his brother, who was a professor at UCLA, for help in the idea. His brother rented servers in the United States for him, upon which the new company would operate. He offered more than 25 percent of the company to people who were going to work with him on the website—in technology, in operations, in sales and marketing, and to a board advisor. Nobody got a salary, quite simply because there was no money to pay anyone. The new team wasted no time; in just three days, they had 1000 jobs ready to post on the site; within a week, a server, and another week's time, a website was ready for launch. Naukri.com was fully operational by March 1997.

It wasn't long before the site started getting press coverage—the Indian job market was big news—and the site began building traffic. Revenues increased nearly ninefold that first year, and suddenly naukri. com was Info Edge's biggest revenue generator. Sanjeev put all of his resources into the venture. He believed it would be the company's future, but he was still afraid that it might fail. Sanjeev says most managers never really understand that level of risk, because they have never lived with the personal fear of losing everything they have (or love). To deal with fear, he says you have to be able to dissect the risk, to understand it, to face it, and to mitigate it, without losing sight of your goal.

Being an entrepreneur, Sanjeev says, is about taking leaps of faith—often several leaps a day—and doing what "feels right" even if that goes against what others say or believe. For Sanjeev, it demands perseverance and the ability to accept failure as part of the process. To him, failure teaches you not only what you are doing wrong, but also how to do it right the next time. He says, "It's a useful, if not transformational, force," adding confidently that "for the entrepreneur, failure is not only inevitable, it's a way of life."

Sanjeev also believes in searching for meaning, not money, in one's work. He asks himself, "What can I do that will outlive me? Why am I here? What are my passions? What is my calling?" If you can find the meaning, he says the money will come. And it did.

In 1999, the investment bankers began calling. At first, Sanjeev resisted because he wanted to maintain control of his company. But when a new and well-funded competitor (jobsahead.com) began gaining market share, Sanjeev reconsidered. He and his management team agreed to take funding from ICICI Venture in April 2000. That turned out to be an important decision, especially when the dot-com bubble burst just a few months later. But it was Sanjeev's frugal mindset and strategic decision making that helped the company get through tough times. He and the leadership team made judicious investments in technology, products, people, offices, and market development, all while slowly paying off debt.

In 2006, Info Edge became the first purely Indian dot-com company to conduct a successful IPO and be publicly traded on an Indian stock exchange. Today, this small but mighty Delhi-based company employs nearly 2,500 associates and generates more than $75 million in revenue, with a market cap of about $650 million. Through continual innovation and attention to market needs, Naukri.com has expanded to offer an executive search service, a matrimony site (perfect for a country where arranged marriages are still quite common), a social networking platform, and most recently a job website for the Middle East known as naukrigulf.com.

Sanjeev has defined a new model for globalisation. Unlike many of the other executives profiled in the book who are leading Western-based companies that have expanded their global presence to customize offerings for emerging markets, Sanjeev has always served the Indian market by drawing upon the resources of the rest of the world. He relies on the U.S. technology backbone for his operational infrastructure. He leverages capital markets in the U.S., Europe, India, and Asia. He calls on international business and financial analysts to advise him on global trends, and he builds market share with multinational companies looking for talent in India. Sanjeev has figured out how to leverage the power of a global ecosystem to serve customers at home and around the world with minimal complexity in his business model, organizational structure, and operations. He adds: "Complex companies forget what they are good at. At naukri.com, we never want to forget what we are good at. I never want to forget what I am good at."

He admits, he is not an expert at anything—except, perhaps, surrounding himself with the best of the best. And when he has made mistakes, Sanjeev says it is because he did not listen to his partners, to his people. As he has matured, Sanjeev says he listens…and listens…and listens. A global leader, in his opinion, can never listen too much.

An engaging conversationalist with an infectious energy level, there is no question how and why he is the company's best salesperson—he can sell "trust" across the table. By being trustworthy himself, Sanjeev has an exceptional ability to inspire and attract good people to work for his company, customers to buy his services, and investors to put money behind his business. "If you can do this," he says, "you can persuade people to invest their time or their money or their intelligence in your company." Sanjeev has a sense of fairness you can feel, and people are willing to work hard for him in return. This worked when he first gave shares of his fledgling company to his very first employees, and it continues today as he builds out a network of customers and business partners. Because his company operates in the virtual world, Sanjeev relies on real people who can build quality relationships with customers, investors, and business partners.

Sanjeev's growth strategy is to identify customer needs in markets where there is not already a dominant player and where he can achieve first-mover advantage. He believes you make money not just by performing a valuable task but by serving your core customers better and more profitably than your competitors. "The sharper your differentiation," he says, "the greater your advantage." To hear him explain it, differentiation is easy: "We understand what's abundant and what's scarce."

Sanjeev is optimistic about the future of his country. A more educated and highly motivated younger generation is driving much of the growth in the country, and he hopes to contribute to that trend as one of the early founders of Ashoka University (IFRE), a liberal arts school in Delhi modeled off the U.S. college system. In collaboration with the University of Pennsylvania, IFRE is designed to provide a common platform for dialogue and action on new ideas and innovation in higher education through active engagement with students, parents, academicians, plus social and business leaders. Sanjeev hopes to make liberal arts a centerpiece of higher learning in India.

Despite his optimism, Sanjeev admits the political landscape in India makes it difficult for businesses that deal with the government to operate in a highly ethical manner. Government regulation is central to doing business in India, and business leaders must have a sophisticated appreciation of the dynamics in order to navigate what can be a corrupt landscape. He made the commitment early on to run his company as a clean business; an admirable ambition, but one that has at times limited his options in certain business sectors. Because he wanted to do business by the book, Sanjeev has deliberately walked away from certain business sectors and opportunities. Ethical behavior transcends legal compliance, says Sanjeev: "It's about satisfying one's conscience, whereas legal compliance is about merely satisfying the authorities."

When I asked Sanjeev about the most important lesson he has learned on this journey, he reflects on those inflection points that changed his life: when he passed up going to IIT, when he relied on his wife for income, when he spent more time working and less than he wanted to with family. Through it all, Sanjeev has stayed true to his course, adding, "If you go through inflection shifts early in life—and often enough—you can learn and grow and benefit from them, if you pay attention." As he nears 50, he is experiencing yet another inflection point. He notes that this is the time in an executive's career when focus shifts from future to past. "And when one begins to realize that the most significant events may have happened behind—not in front—of me." But through it all, Sanjeev remains committed to himself, his family, his company, and his country. And having a chance to know Sanjeev, I can only imagine the best is yet to come.

GOING THE DISTANCE

Frits van Paasschen
CEO Starwood Hotels & Resorts Worldwide Inc.

Frits van Paasschen knows how to go the distance. With dozens of endurance events, marathons, 48-hour running relays, and triathlons under his belt, Frits understands what it takes to set high personal goals, to overcome personal fears and breakthrough barriers, and then to do it all over again. He applies that same approach to his role as CEO of Starwood Hotels & Resorts Worldwide. With long-standing iconic names like Sheraton, hip and personal service brands like W, and newcomers like the more affordable Aloft line of hotels in Starwood's portfolio, the company is growing fast and has aggressive expansion plans around the world. Frits recognizes that driving global growth—especially in emerging markets—is centered on leveraging the perspectives of his leadership team around the world. To put this concept into a runner's vernacular: He knows he has a lot of different style runners on his team, but they all need to reach the same finish line as top performers in their class.

Frits is one of those CEOs who is accessible, smart, well-versed, and easy to talk with on almost any subject. You get the sense that communication across borders and boundaries comes very naturally to him. But he also knows that just because something might be painfully clear to him, he must take the time to share his vision with the rest of his team and, more importantly, to bring them into the dialogue. Unlike many executives in his position, he spends a considerable amount of time documenting his ideas and the thought process around them, which makes him an exceptional communicator. Those who work for him say his willingness (and courage) to share what he is thinking makes him far more accessible to the organization than many CEOs. It not only helps them understand where the company is going and why, but it also helps to validate his decisions, to gain an appreciation for other ways of looking at a problem or opportunity, and to ultimately achieve the optimum outcome. At times, he even takes different points of view, just to challenge the obvious answer. In this way, Frits intentionally creates an environment for great decisions to be made.

But just knowing where you want to go isn't enough. You also need the right kind of training. If you are running a race, you can train in the gym, but you eventually need to try out the actual course. That's why Frits has instituted leadership initiatives like Starwood Leadership 100 (profiled in chapter 6) that enable his team to experience firsthand the markets that are critical to the company's growth strategy. Two-thirds of the properties Starwood plans to open in 2013 will be in the world's fastest growing travel markets. Today, Asia accounts for 25 percent of Starwood's existing hotel rooms, but more than half of the company's pipeline. That's why he relocated his company's headquarters and entire executive team to China for a month in 2011 and is relocating his team to Dubai in 2013. As Frits describes it, "You don't really know a market until you buy groceries there and it's difficult to do that if you are just visiting." Frits believes in the power of symbolic events. Taking the team to China for an extended stay was not about trying to run the business *from* China, but rather to draw attention to the importance of the Chinese market, and to build Starwood as a global brand.

At the time, Starwood was undergoing unprecedented growth in China, with 100 hotels in operation and another 100 under construction. The company had also launched a personalized China travel program. Frits explains that many things the team learned during its extended stay in China made it stronger and smarter. The Chinese experience underscored the importance of adapting to local travel preferences while staying true to Starwood's brand promise. It also generated significant brand awareness among a rapidly growing population of Chinese travelling to other regions of the world. Outbound travel from China continues to grow at a double digit pace and in 2012, 95 percent of Starwood properties welcomed guests from Greater China.

As a result of successful China relocation, Starwood's executive team moved to Dubai for a month in March 2013. The goal was to further strengthen Starwood's global vantage and to bring Frits and his executive team closer to key growth markets. Dubai is the perfect choice for this type of immersion, as it's fast becoming an important global travel destination and hub. That's reflected in Starwood's presence in the city, where there are 14 Starwood hotels—second only to New York City.

With global executive experience working for companies such as Disney, Nike, and Molson Coors, Frits understands the power of a global brand. His goal since becoming CEO in 2007 is to make Starwood as synonymous with global lifestyle hotel brands as Coca Cola is with soft drinks and Google is with search engines. As Frits explains it, "Branding position in this industry is unique. The brand itself is about the experience as opposed to image or personal identification. In a consumer business, you can redefine your product mix season by season. It is pretty hard to do when you have literally billions of dollars of real estate to try to move. The challenge is to be nimble in some ways and yet to be patient in others." In other words, Frits has to have a team that can excel at the endurance competition.

Frits, himself, is a global nomad. He manages the company by flying around. Over the past four years, Frits has visited more than 400 of the chain's hotels in more than 100 cities in 40 countries. While he can personally observe what is happening in these markets, it also provides an opportunity to engage local leadership in the company's broader vision and strategy. This, he believes, creates a multiplier effect. Not only does he have more minds contributing to a better strategy, he also has more disciples spreading the word around the globe.

The ability to personally engage, to drop in and be a part of the community and the culture is critically important to Frits. Frits speaks five languages fluently, and is working on his sixth. He strives to speak the local language, even if he is not proficient. He believes it shows respect for the local culture, taking him off the CEO pedestal and involving him in real conversations. Some things, he says, you just cannot understand if you do not know how language is expressed. This inclination and willingness may be the result of how he was raised and with his parents' personal challenges and triumphs.

Both his parents spent time as children in Japanese internment camps in Indonesia during World War II. They moved to America from the Netherlands to give Frits and his sister better, safer lives. Frits says this explains a lot of his drive to succeed. His father was a pediatrician, his mother a biomedical researcher who specialized in kidney dialysis. Frits recalls seeing his mother often dismissed in day-to-day interactions because her English was not perfect. For this reason, he strives to treat everyone with respect.

For Frits, it is always about learning something new in order to excel in different ways. When he considered the job at Starwood, Fritz asked himself if it would teach him something he did not already know— if it would put him in a position where he would be challenged. He says that is certainly the case for a company that not only operates globally but also has significant assets spread around the world.

Frits and his leadership team must stay vigilant when it comes to the forces of globalisation that are shifting economic, power, and trade patterns from the Western to the developing world. With 70 percent of the world's economic growth expected to be in emerging markets, traditional leaders must be able to interpret the world events and act upon them much more quickly than ever before.

Sustainability is a critical issue for Starwood. Frits says it's no longer a matter of doing good, but of doing what is urgently needed. With greenhouse gas concentrations rising and climate change already having devastating impacts, he says consumers want to buy from greener companies. Under Frits' leadership, Starwood seeks to reduce energy consumption by 30 percent by 2020. He is tapping into his employees for their ideas on how to reduce the company's carbon footprint, while actively engaging customers with incentives to recycle and reduce water usage.

In a call to action in early 2012, Frits outlined what he described as a new kind of leadership for changing times and offered five *thought starters* for his team to embrace:

Be Here. Be Present. Senior executives need to know what is going on around the world, even if it is exhausting and consumes much of what many other executives consider free time, such as weekends. For Frits, showing up is not enough, you need to actively listen and be ready to reach across cultures and languages.

A Simpler Strategy. Because the core business is harder to manage than it was just a decade ago, Frits says Starwood must continually redefine strategy to strive to do what it does better than any other company on earth. As a matter of course, Frits asks himself "Am I doing something now that only I can do (or I can do better) to create value?"

A Little More Conversation. Communicating strategy takes a great deal of work, especially when it requires reaching many markets and cultures. The core message needs to be the same, but you need to adjust what you say, the tone, and the points to emphasize for associates, investors, partners, time zones, or media. He adds that CEOs need to realize the power of informal, ongoing dialogue. "It always trumps PowerPoint in the boardroom."

Be Self-Skeptical. Frits cautions his leaders to be skeptical, not just about what people tell them, but also about what they tell themselves. Assumptions are rooted in cultural upbringings and in a personal sense about how the world has worked up until now. Remember, the world is changing and the power is shifting.

The Importance of Being Earnest. Frits stresses the importance of understanding your own moral code, what drives you. And he draws upon the values he learned from his own parents, including having a clear sense of right and wrong and seeing effort as more important than talent. As he explains, "If you believe that talent matters more than effort, you will view each failure as an indictment of your talent rather than an invitation to learn and do better next time."

REAL VALUE FROM MONEY TAKES REAL LEADERSHIP

Hikmet Ersek

President and Chief Executive Officer, Western Union

Western Union is an iconic brand, known around the world as the money transfer company, but for CEO Hikmet Ersek, being well-known primarily for doing one thing very well is one of the biggest challenges he faces as he seeks to reinvent the 162 year-old company. In addition to finding new ways for the company to leverage its core competency, which is moving money around, he wants to change how the rest of the world views Western Union, especially the investment community that has questioned the long-term viability of what has been essentially an old business model.

Lead for the Long-Run

Hikmet doesn't make excuses—that's one of his core strengths, including his transparency and his authenticity. He readily admits the consumer-to-consumer money transfer business has slowed, especially in more economically challenged regions such as Europe and in increasingly competitive markets such as Mexico. But he does this in the context of a much greater vision for how the company must undergo significant change to meet evolving market needs. This requires significant investments in digital and mobile technology, in acquisitions, and in leadership competencies, which have not always come easily. Six months into the CEO role, Hikmet oversaw a highly debated acquisition of Travelex

Global Business Payments, which gave what had been a primarily customer-to-customer (C2C) company significantly greater capabilities in business-to-business (B2B) marketplaces. It was a big purchase—$1 billion worth—in a still weak economy, but as in everything Hikmet does, he fully believes it's the right thing to do, despite his critics: "I have had a few sleepless nights over the last few months. My credibility and my management decisions were questioned. But my duty and my goal are to long-term shareholder value. I was willing to take a large amount of money off market cap, but we are doing the right thing for the long term. I believe in our vision. My management team believes in our vision. And most importantly, our customers believe in our vision." A self-aware executive, he knows his work is complex, and he appreciates the risk involved—he could be fired if he fails—but his strength of conviction is another reason why Hikmet epitomizes a truly global leader.

Perhaps more than any other leader I have worked with, Hikmet has a level of comfort with the uncomfortable, a sensibility that he is trying to develop in the company itself. He started with the leadership team, which, with the exception of the CFO, has completely turned over in the past two years. As an example, he says if it ever makes sense to stop sending telegrams—the business that put Western Union on the map—he needs a team that can make the hard decisions. Hikmet also admits he doesn't know everything and that's why he hires the kind of people who can take the business to the next level. That's why the CFO, who Hikmet credits with the idea for expanding the organization's digital offerings and capabilities, is still on the team.

Hikmet is a team player, a skill he no doubt honed during his tenure as a semi-professional basketball player. He is a relationship-oriented executive, bringing his trusted advisers close in, not unlike a sports huddle, to understand their perspectives and benefit from their insights.

The team mentality has also positioned Hikmet well for building an ecosystem around the entire value chain in order to drive Western Union's success in three growth areas:

- expansion of its global consumer financial services

- further development of its B2B capabilities to serve small- and medium-sized enterprises and specific markets such as higher education and nongovernmental organizations (NGOs)
- new ventures including stored value (for example, prepaid cards) and creating insights from data around how money moves.

In addition to several acquisitions beyond the Travelex purchase, Hikmet and his team have created partnerships with proven innovators: Ericsson, Allianz, and MasterCard.

Ericsson, another century-plus old company that is quickly becoming a mobile market leader, will help accelerate the launch of Western Union's mobile financial services to consumers around the world.

The global integrated insurance and asset management firm, Allianz, joined with Western Union to explore how to deliver more financial services to markets that otherwise would not have access to banking or insurance products or services.

Under a partnership designed to build the world's largest global stored-value network, MasterCard will be the preferred brand for Western Union-sponsored prepaid programs around the world and Western Union the preferred money-transfer provider for MasterCard.

With each of these alliances, Hikmet seeks to make Western Union the premier financial service provider for those with unmet financial needs, a market he estimates to be at least 2 billion people strong. But his vision is not just about strategy and economic opportunity, it's about narrowing the economic gaps between rich and poor. And in doing so, he can empower local communities, not only by employing people as part of the Western Union agent partner network, which has grown fivefold since Hikmet joined the company in the late 1990s, but also by providing practical products for local residents. As Hikmet explains it, "The needs of the underserved are the same as billionaires: They want to be treated with financial dignity. I want to create social value for these people...I want my company to be part of it."

This is a very personal mission for Hikmet. Born of an Austrian (Christian) mother and Turkish (Muslim) father, Hikmet grew up in his father's home of Istanbul. "I've been sending him money for medicine and other needs every week for years, from whatever country I'm in. My father has a cell phone but doesn't use it. Before I became CEO, he had to walk a mile or two to the closest Western Union agent. Now there's one much closer, and thousands of other people can send and receive funds in several ways" (2012).

Western Union is a truly global company, with more than 500,000 locations in more than 200 countries and territories, and Hikmet has been to most of them. But not as an insulated executive. He explains: "I will go to places that most executives won't go—and will spend hours and hours with my employees in the markets being with our customers. I won't protect myself from the reality of our markets. I come from here—so I am not afraid of it."

Deep market understanding and an appreciation for diversity are core competencies for Hikmet that he is trying to increase within the company. When he launched Western Union Digital Ventures, he purposefully recruited his head of the Africa business to be the lead executive because he wanted someone who fully grasped the dynamics of one of the major geographic regions the new enterprise is designed to serve. And he was equally deliberate in the selection of San Francisco as the location for the global headquarters. In addition to wanting to draw upon the talents of the Bay area, the decision was a symbolic gesture, signaling a desire to create a new culture. Hikmet even goes so far as to require headquarters employees who want to visit the San Francisco office to "apply" to him for permission, not for the purposes of controlling access, but rather to limit the potential for them to infuse the legacy corporate culture into the new operation.

Going Digital

While Western Union Digital Ventures currently only represents fewer than 5 percent of total company revenue, it is experiencing double-digit growth. Hikmet believes "it will be the future of the business," but he continues to balance these opportunities with the need to take care of the core business. Leadership for Hikmet requires a combination of seemingly incompatible qualities:

- an analytical mind that can zoom in on the financial details and business processes to identify opportunities for improvements—something he learned early on in his days at GE
- courage to act and act fast, even in the face of painful feedback
- creativity, imagination, and a passion for the needs of the customer.

Like so many of the other executives profiled, Hikmet recognizes the potential he has as a CEO. But he has a much deeper appreciation for the power of his position. Early in his career, Hikmet says he sought power for power's sake. Now he wants power to create good. He says leaders need to be very thoughtful and respectful of the power they have achieved and not get caught up in what they think (or others say) they should be or do in their roles, another sign of Hikmet's authentic nature.

Hikmet has been able to bring together his skills to build market value and his passion for the underserved with Western Union Social Ventures. To him it makes perfect business sense. As he put it: "Shareholder value only happens when you satisfy the customer." He realizes that if Western Union can package its offerings to meet their needs, he can do both: meet social needs and build market value. Under his leadership, Western Union launched the social ventures department, which among other things is helping NGOs send funds directly to those in need, reducing the risk that they will end up in the hands of corrupt government officials before they can reach their intended recipients.

This ability to link both comes from Hikmet's driving desire to understand the underlying cause of a problem and the long-term solutions. Ask his senior leaders and they will tell you he is constantly asking "why," mapping the possibilities by asking questions about what will support the current business margins while seeking additional growth opportunities in new markets.

While he asks why, he also explains why. According to the former president of the Western Union Foundation: "Hikmet is the first Western Union CEO who underscores the true meaning of our business: about the business being of a higher purpose, of using our products to change lives and solve social problems."

Only time will tell if he is successful, but Hikmet remains committed to his strategy and his purpose. He is leveraging the company's brand and worldwide distribution network, investing in new technologies, markets, and partnerships, and challenging his employees, his board, and his shareholders. Not an easy path to take. But knowing Hikmet, he could take no other. After all, he is out to change the world.

THE HEART AND MIND OF LEADERSHIP

Maya Strelar-Migotti

Head of Silicon Valley Site and Vice President, IP and
Broadband Development, Ericsson

Maya Strelar-Migotti exemplifies many of the seemingly contradictory attributes that those leading on the edge must embrace in a globally connected, yet highly diverse business environment. Educated as an electrical engineer, Maya has held numerous positions with Ericsson since joining the telecommunications giant in 1987, including head of product management for mobile services and applications, vice president of engineering unit IP networks, and earlier as a software developer and in customer support. Today, as the executive lead for the company's IP and Broadband development unit, Maya is responsible for a distributed organization with more than 6,000 people working in 18 different locations around the globe.

A results-oriented, metrics-driven executive, Maya is at home at Ericsson, which is known for its culture of performance and measurement. Born in Croatia, an only child of former political prisoners, Maya set her goals early: to graduate from college and to move to the free world. She accomplished her goal, moving to Australia in 1988, when she was able to secure a green card. She followed her husband to Spain in 1991 when he was offered a job there and soon after assumed her first managerial role with Ericsson. Four years later she moved to the company's headquarters in Sweden, where she began building her professional network and learning the corporate culture.

Ericsson is all about statistics, which give the company the ability to understand at any given point in time how the company or a specific business unit is performing. Maya says Ericsson is "top of the game" in this regard. Apparently, it works. After more than 135 years in business, Ericsson is the world's largest maker of equipment for building mobile telecommunications networks. When discussing metrics and their importance, Maya laughs as she explains: "If you don't know how much you weigh, how can you know how much you need to lose?"

It's this very personal approach that makes Maya successful running such a large organization and in an industry that has seen revolutionary change with the explosion of the mobile Internet. She understands what drives people, despite their differences, and what it takes to get to the numbers the company needs. Too often, she says, companies and their leaders put too little emphasis on the cultural aspects of running a globally dispersed organization. They think culture is a very soft concept in the business world, but Maya says creating a culture of trust, transparency, and respect is what it takes to achieve the very hard and impressive performance levels Ericsson requires, and that she as an executive delivers.

This is a lesson she first learned in 2003, when she found herself as the vice president of a development unit with 1,000 engineers scattered around the world, most of whom had never worked with one another before. Along the way, they had developed different technologies and different processes, and now, under Maya's leadership, they had to learn how to get their systems—and themselves—to work together. As she faced this challenge, she recalled a time years ago in Spain when she noticed that all of the sunflowers in a field were pointed in the same direction: toward the sun. She asked herself, how do I make those in my organization do the same, to share the same vision and goals and definition of what success looks like?

When she thought about it, Maya realized it was quite simple and logical, though it is a point many leaders miss: You start by telling them, and you keep communicating, using all of the technological resources at your disposal. More importantly, you create an environment of open dialogue where you can gather feedback and encourage informal thought leadership. Maya says communication is fundamental to building the levels of trust and alignment necessary to build seamless teams that can deliver as if they were all sitting in the same building.

While Maya runs a very diverse team, she understands what people have in common: They all want to know why the company, the division, and their work team are doing what they are doing, how decisions are being made, and where they expect to be as they move forward. As a leader who answers these questions, Maya brings purpose to the members of her organization and to their work. Creating common goals and providing people with the opportunity to be proud of their successes is the aligning factor.

This was the thinking behind Ericsson's approach to innovation in her development unit, which has reached new frontiers under Maya's leadership. In 2010, she gave her newly appointed head of innovation, Gabriel Broner, an open invitation and opportunity to make the IP and broadband development unit—and all 6000 of its employees—much more innovative. The result was the highly successful Ericsson Innova program, which provides venture capital-like funding to help employees transform their ideas into reality and design thinking methodology to sustain innovation. Design thinking brought the company closer to its customers' needs, while the company's open recognition and respect for the innovative process—with all of its starts, stops, and setbacks— keeps people inspired to work on solutions to meaningful problems.

Within just two years, the program, which is designed to "bring Silicon Valley-style innovation inside Ericsson," had received more than 2,000 ideas, 200 of which were funded, more than 20 beyond the initial round. The company estimates the first three ideas alone generated $20 million in software revenue and productivity improvements. Broner says that without Maya's "courage and vision to request, sponsor, and continually support this initiative, Ericsson Innova would not have happened."

For Maya, it's about putting structure around innovation, which to many seems contradictory, but she says is necessary in a company the size and complexity of Ericsson. She uses a similar approach to create a winning culture in her organization, complete with frameworks around leadership behavior, governance, strategy deployment and, of course, scorecards to measure success. If Ericsson is to continue its winning streak in an increasingly competitive and highly dynamic marketplace, Maya says she has to have winning teams internally. She supports their success by sharing her vision, providing avenues for feedback, and giving people an opportunity to make a positive difference. For example, one of the principles behind Ericsson Innova's success is its ability to attract "people who want to innovate because they are passionate about their ideas and want to see them through" as opposed to those just motivated by "a pot of money." As Maya describes it, when people understand and agree with the goals of the company and the positive results that can be achieved, they work harder. In other words, people increase their commitment when you "touch" their hearts. But when you bring the brain and heart together, she says, you achieve even more amazing results.

References

Anthony, S.D. (2012). "The New Corporate Garage." *Harvard Business Review*. Retrieved from http://hbr.org/2012/09/the-new-corporate-garage/ar/1.

Aulakh, G. (2012). "Cisco Systems to Raise India Staff By 60 Percent Over Next Four Years." *The Economic Times*.

Barone, S.G. (2010). "Psychographics vs. Demographics: Which Is What and When Is It Better?" Barodine Marketing. Retrieved from http://www.ebarodine.com/test.2.html.

Bennis, W. (2012). "Minding the Gap: Nohria's MBA Reforms at Harvard." *Businessweek*. Retrieved from http://www.businessweek.com/articles/2012-07-23/minding-the-gap-nohrias-mba-reforms-at-harvard#p1.

Berger, D.M. (1987). *Clinical Empathy*. Northvale, New Jersey: Jason Aronson.

Bossidy, L. (2001). "The Job No CEO Should Delegate." *Harvard Business Review*. Retrieved from http://hbr.org/2001/03/the-job-no-ceo-should-delegate/ar/1.

Bronson, P., and A. Merryman. (2010). "The Creativity Crisis." *Newsweek*. Retrieved from http://www.thedailybeast.com/newsweek/2010/07/10/the-creativity-crisis.html.

Carr, D. (2013). "Interview with Fareed Zakaria." *United Hemispheres Inflight Magazine*. Retrieved from http://www.hemispheresmagazine.com/2013/02/01/the-hemi-qa-fareed-zakaria/.

CBS Interactive. (2013). "Design Innovator 'Schools' Charlie Rose." *60 Minutes*. Retrieved from http://www.cbsnews.com/8301-18560_162-57562097/design-innovator-schools-charlie-rose/.

Covey, S.M.R. (2010). "Interview With Stephen M.R. Covey." *CNN*. Retrieved from http://speedoftrust.com/new/resources/news-media/.

Creating Minds.org. (2010). "Age and Creativity." Retrieved from http://creatingminds.org/articles/age.htm.

Crompton, S. (2008). *All About Me: Loving a Narcissist*. New York: HarperCollins.

Dan, A. (2012). "In a VUCA World, Unilever Bets on 'Sustainable Living' as a Transformative Business Model." *Forbes*. Retrieved from http://www.forbes.com/sites/avidan/2012/10/14/in-a-vuca-world-unilever-bets-on-sustainable-living-as-a-transformative-business-model/.

Ersek, H. (2012). "A Spectrum of Traditions." *The New York Times*. Retrieved from http://www.nytimes.com/2012/07/29/jobs/hikmet-ersek-of-western-union-and-a-spectrum-of-tradition.html?_r=0.

Fisher, C.J. (2000). "Like It or Not...Culture Matters." Fisher Consulting Group. Retrieved from http://fisherconsultinggroup.com/uploads/articles/Culture%20Matters%20Article%20-%209.07.pdf.

Gast, A., and M. Zanini. (2012). "The Social Side of Strategy." McKinsey & Company. Retrieved from http://www.mckinsey.com/insights/strategy/the_social_side_of_strategy.

Goleman, D. (2004). "What Makes a Leader?" *Harvard Business Review*. Retrieved from http://hbr.org/2004/01/what-makes-a-leader.

Hagel, J.III, and J.S. Brown. (2012). *The Power of Pull: How Small Moves, Smartly Made, Can Set Big Things in Motion*. New York: Basic Books.

Harth, C. (2013). "GSF Fact Sheet 1: The State of Global Studies in the United States." Global Studies Foundation. Retrieved from http://www.globalstudiesfoundation.org/publications.cfm?id=2.

Hempel, J. (2006). "The Collective Wisdom of Crowds Depends on Your Crowd, and IBM." *Businessweek*. Retrieved from www.businessweek.com/stories/2006-08-06/big-blue-brainstorm.

International Monetary Fund. (2012). "World Economic and Financial Surveys." Retrieved from http://www.imf.org/external/pubs/ft/weo/2012/01/weodata/index.aspx.

Kiechel, W. (2012). "The Management Century." *Harvard Business Review*. Retrieved from http://hbr.org/product/the-management-century/an/R1211C-PDF-ENG.

Lashinsky, A. (2012). "Amazon's Jeff Bezos: The Ultimate Disrupter." *CNN Money*. Retrieved from http://management.fortune.cnn.com/2012/11/16/jeff-bezos-amazon/.

Maccoby, M. (2003). *The Productive Narcissist: The Promise and Peril of Visionary Leadership*. New York: Broadway Books.

Maddison, A. (2001). *The World Economy: A Millennial Perspective*. Paris: OECD.

Malloy, C. (2012). "Wall Street Doesn't Understand Innovation." *Harvard Business Review*. Retrieved from http://hbr.org/2012/12/wall-street-doesnt-understand-innovation/ar/1.

Martin, R.L. (2007). *The Opposable Mind: How Successful Leaders Win Through Integrative Thinking*. Boston: Harvard Business School Press.

McIlvaine, A.R. (2010). "The Leadership Factor." *Human Resource Executive Online*. Retrieved from http://www.hreonline.com/HRE/story.jsp?storyId=330860027.

Mitchell, C., R.L. Ray, and B. van Ark. (2012). *The Conference Board CEO Challenge 2012: Risky Business—Focusing on Innovation and Talent in a Volatile World*. The Conference Board.

National Science Foundation. (2010). *Science and Engineering Indicators: 2010*. Retrieved from http://www.nsf.gov/statistics/seind10/c2/c2s5.htm.

Neal, A. and R. Kovach. (2010). "Performance Management That the CEO Cares About." In *The Executive Guide to Integrated Talent Management*, eds. Oakes, K., and P. Galagan. Alexandria, VA: ASTD Press.

Nova ScienceNOW. (2012). "Foldit and EteRNA." Retrieved from http://www.youtube.com/watch?v=bTlNNFQxs_A.

Nussbaum, B. (2009). "Life in Beta—How Design Thinking Can Help Us Navigate Through This Time of Cascading Change." *Businessweek*. Retrieved from http://www.businessweek.com/innovate/NussbaumOnDesign/archives/2009/11/life_in_beta--how_design_thinking_can_help_us_navigate_through_this_time_of_cascading_change.html.

Patel, P. (2010). "Outsourcing's Education Gap." IEEE Spectrum. Retrieved from http://spectrum.ieee.org/at-work/tech-careers/outsourcings-education-gap.

Puiu, T. (2011). "Gamers Solve Decade-Old HIV Puzzle in 10 Days." ZME Science. Retrieved from http://www.zmescience.com/research/studies/gamers-solve-decade-old-hiv-puzzle-in-ten-days/.

Raman, A.P. (2011). "Why Don't We Try to Be India's Most Respected Company?: An Interview with N.R. Narayana Murthy." *Harvard Business Review*.

Rose, C. (2012). "Jeff Bezos, Founder and CEO, Amazon.com." Retrieved from http://www.charlierose.com/search/?text=Jeff+Bezos.

Shapiro, S. (2008). "Do We Get Less Creative As We Age?" Retrieved from http://www.steveshapiro.com/2008/02/07/do-we-get-less-creative-as-we-age/.

------. (2013). *Steven Shapiro's 24/7 Innovation*. Retrieved from http://www.steveshapiro.com/.

Tavangar, H.S. (2009). *Growing Up Global: Raising Children to Be at Home in the World*. New York: Ballantine Books.

Telecom Regulatory Authority of India. (2012). "Highlights on Telecom Subscription Data as on 31st May 2012." Retrieved from http://www.trai.gov.in/WriteReadData/PressRealease/Document/PR-TSD-May12.pdf.

Wolverson, R. (2013). "The TIME at Davos Debate: The Rewards of Mastering Risk." *Time Online*. Retrieved from http://business.time.com/2013/01/25/the-time-at-davos-debate-the-rewards-of-mastering-risk/.

About the Author

Dr. Annmarie Neal is a world-renowned business executive, thought leader, author, and speaker on the topics of business strategy, innovative talent management, and executive leadership. She has specific expertise in organizations in transformation where disruption of contemporary business and leadership models is required. She is internationally recognized for positioning companies to achieve growth objectives and commercial success through innovating organizational culture and reinventing executive leadership. With more than 20 years of global experience leading organizations and consulting with global business presidents and senior executives across a range of industries, she powerfully translates her expertise across multiple industries, life cycles, and geographies. She takes a decidedly business-centric and global approach, translating business objectives into winning talent strategies. She thrives in the complexity of high-growth businesses where fast-paced change and innovation are critical to the company's success.

Annmarie is currently the founder of the Center for Leadership Innovation. Previously she has held the chief talent officer role in both Cisco Systems and First Data Corporation. She has served on several advisory boards, including the University of Colorado's Business School, the Center for Work-Life Policy, ASTD, TruEffect, and SoftServe, Inc. She is also a senior fellow and researcher with the Corporate Leadership Board.

She received her doctorate in clinical psychology, with an emphasis in management psychology, from the California School of Professional Psychology Alameda/Berkeley. She holds a master's degree in counseling from Santa Clara University, a graduate certificate of special studies from Harvard University, and a bachelor's degree from Boston College.

She lives in Colorado where she enjoys skiing, golfing, running half-marathons, and spending time with her 10 year-old son. She can be reached at annmarie@centerforleadershipinnovation.com and followed on twitter @nealannmarie.

Karen Conway is a frequently requested international speaker and author, especially on the topic of how collaboration and alignment across diverse stakeholders can drive industry transformation. She is at ease moderating large-scale discussions on healthcare reform between Senators Tom Daschle and Bill Frist, as she is while building consensus among environmentalists and oil and gas producers. Conway has held executive positions in healthcare and energy and has extensive experience in government and public affairs, print journalism, and as a radio and television talk show host. Her firm Conway Associates created a unique approach to strategic communication based on her father's firsthand experience working with Dr. W. Edwards Deming and Procter & Gamble. Conway's work has appeared in *Redbook*, *USA Today*, *Parenting*, and also in books published by Springer in London.

Index

C

G

H

HOW TO PURCHASE ASTD PRESS PRODUCTS

All ASTD Press titles may be purchased through ASTD's online store at **www.store.astd.org**.

ASTD Press products are available worldwide through various outlets and booksellers. In the United States and Canada, individuals may also purchase titles (print or eBook) from:

Amazon– www.amazon.com (USA); www.amazon.com (CA)
Google Play– play.google.com/store
EBSCO– www.ebscohost.com/ebooks/home

Outside the United States, English-language ASTD Press titles may be purchased through distributors (divided geographically).

United Kingdom, Continental Europe, the Middle East, North Africa, Central Asia, and Latin America:
Eurospan Group
Phone: 44.1767.604.972
Fax: 44.1767.601.640
Email: eurospan@turpin-distribution.com
Web: www.eurospanbookstore.com
For a complete list of countries serviced via Eurospan please visit www.store.astd.org or email publications@astd.org.

South Africa:
Knowledge Resources
Phone: +27(11)880-8540
Fax: +27(11)880-8700/9829
Email: mail@knowres.co.za
Web: http://www.kr.co.za
For a complete list of countries serviced via Knowledge Resources please visit www.store.astd.org or email publications@astd.org.

Nigeria:
Paradise Bookshops
Phone: 08033075133
Email: paradisebookshops@gmail.com
Website: www.paradisebookshops.com

Asia:
Cengage Learning Asia Pte. Ltd.
Email: asia.info@cengage.com
Web: www.cengageasia.com
For a complete list of countries serviced via Cengage Learning please visit www.store.astd.org or email publications@astd.org.

India:
Cengage India Pvt. Ltd.
Phone: 011 43644 1111
Fax: 011 4364 1100
Email: asia.infoindia@cengage.com

For all other countries, customers may send their publication orders directly to ASTD. Please visit: **www.store.astd.org**.